WOK & CO

Ken Hom

Mickaël Roulier • Giacomo Bretzel

WOK & CO

Ken Hom

Mickaël Roulier • Giacomo Bretzel

translation and editorial collaboration by Sophie Brissaud
photographs by Mickaël Roulier • styling by Emmanuel Turiot
photographs by Giacomo Bretzel

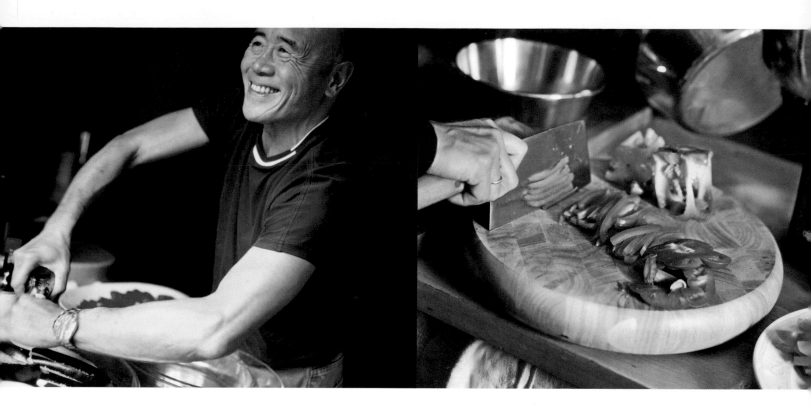

Contents

Introduction

The meeting of East and West is one of the great themes of my life, although I had to reach a certain age before I appreciated the immense breadth of scope it offered. I was born in Tucson, Arizona, in 1949, to Chinese parents. Is it possible to be predominantly Eastern and predominantly Western at the same time? My father died when I was eight years old and my mother took me to live in Chicago, where I spent my childhood and adolescence, nurtured on traditional cooking within the vast network of the close bonds and solidarity that are characteristic of Asian families. Although my mother never remarried, we had plenty of relatives. We were welcomed and integrated into the dependable warmth of a family circle already firmly established in the small Chinese quarter in Chicago.

That is where I grew up, surrounded by my cousins, aunts and uncles, observing all the Chinese customs. In my family we spoke nothing but Chinese. In the afternoon, after attending state school, I went to study at the Chinese school. I was immersed in Chinese culture, Cantonese to be precise. Until very recently, the majority of Chinese immigrants to the United States came from the Guangdong region (of which Canton is the capital). The least that I can say is that my childhood was impregnated, not with the Judaeo-Christian culture, but rather with a typically Chinese cocktail of Confucianism, Taoism and Buddhism according to the following principles: respect for nature, a concern for remaining in constant harmony with nature, and respect for one's family and elders, including one's ancestors. It was only very gradually that I learned to become a real American – that is to say an American with that little something extra.

Like all second generation Americans I am the product of two cultures; however, my Chinese roots have always been profound and indestructible, in the matter of cuisine as well as everything else. This dualism was both the start and the explanation of the path I took. In China, more than anywhere else – except perhaps France, Italy and Thailand – gastronomy is of primary importance. For my mother, my uncles and aunts and my cousins, good food was the favourite topic of conversation. For hours as a child I sat at the table and listened to talk of buying ingredients, preparing them, choosing the dishes for a meal or planning a menu for a special occasion. In Chinese, the phrase *chi fan le mei you*, the equivalent of 'How are you?', means literally, *Have you eaten?* All that seemed perfectly natural at the time, but later, when I became more integrated with North American society, I realized that this kind of conversation happened only rarely. **It was only later, in France, that I found the equivalent of my ancestral gastronomic culture.**

My mother's cooking was supplemented for me by a second initiation to Chinese gastronomy. From the age of eleven I started working part time in my uncle's restaurant. There I learned the rigorous side of this cuisine of which, up to then, I had only known the more agreeable aspects, and I also learned the difference between a galley slave and a young kitchen hand – that is, practically none. For a true appreciation of the delicacy of shrimps one has to have spent hours peeling (shelling) thousands of them. I did this job so many times, pulling handfuls of live shellfish out of jute sacks dripping with sea water!

At the end of the 1960s I was not yet 20 years old. I opted to finish my studies in California. I landed in San Francisco and went to Berkeley, which was one of the most open cities and most tolerant towards Americans of Asian origin and other ethnic minorities. I was filled with enthusiasm for the many restaurants serving specialities from all the regions of China – Canton, of course, but also Sichuan, Hunan, Shanghai, Fujian, etc. – and the abundance, variety and quality of the produce available: fruit, herbs, spices, meat and seafood. This agricultural and gastronomic paradise was not unlike the Cantonese region where my family originated, a veritable land of milk and honey, blessed with unparalleled abundance where everything grows readily and without effort.

From California I went to France and was immediately seduced by the gastronomy of the French regions, and later by that of Italy. I was captivated by the herbs in the gardens of Provence, the markets of the Midi, the vegetables ripened under the hot sun. The delicious, inexpensive meals that I ate in the most improbable of cheap cafés were an absolute delight. My stays in Europe gave my gastronomic culture a considerable boost in the quality department. It was there that I understood the potential offered by the careful combining of ingredients, cooking techniques and cultures. Free from preconceived ideas and mental barriers, I set about furthering my chosen vocation of 'fusionist' cook. French pastries, made with butter, struck me as much lighter than Asian pastries, which are made with lard. On the other hand, Chinese and Japanese mushrooms, with their smoky flavour and strong character, seemed preferable to the sweeter, less flavoursome Western ones. The French version of roast turkey is an improvement on American roast turkey, which is always dry and overcooked, but why not produce an even moister, creamier result by steaming it, as they do in China? And replacing the stuffing of chestnuts and gluey rice by a plum sauce with Chinese spices?

With all these experiences behind me, by the middle of the 1970s I knew that I intended to dedicate my life to cooking. I knew that what I wanted to accomplish – against all commonly accepted opinion – was the merging of East with West via the kitchen. I never felt that this was a misplaced ambition, nor that I was betraying the traditions of either part of the world. Now, after several decades of learning, teaching and practising this culinary 'fusion', I am still as convinced as ever that it was the right path to follow.

I have already mentioned the central role that food plays in Chinese culture: a role that is not only gastronomic but also moral and emotional. My mother and other members of my family instilled this culture into me from a young age, without me being aware of it. When I was a child, one of my uncles, referring one day to a large fish steamed whole, explained that I should never take the cheeks but should leave them for my mother. The cheeks are thought to be the most prized part and filial piety dictated that they went to my mother. It is easy to understand the potential of this culture to awaken nostalgia and dreams in my fellow immigrants. Those of the first generation in my family never became assimilated into the American way of life and clung resolutely to their native language, their native customs and, above all, their native cuisine. The psychological aspect of good food was at its highest when, at the table, the older family members reminisced about the delicious dishes they had eaten in the past. In their dreams they still lived in China and in their daily life they put tremendous effort into reproducing

the flavours, cooking methods and seasonings that they had cherished. There was a constant hunt for ingredients that could be suitable substitutes for Asian products, a profound need to perpetuate the rituals of the kitchen and traditional techniques. *In search of lost tastes.*

The extraordinary adaptability of Chinese cooking came to their aid. Of course, this cuisine is governed by coded and unalterable principles, and certain ingredients – such as dairy products – hardly play any part in it. But it is this very flexible philosophical approach and the simplicity of execution, which has allowed Chinese cooking to win acclaim all over the world. Its basic principles are practical enough to be universal, starting with that of mincing, chopping and cutting up most of the ingredients. That done, sautéing in a wok produces tasty dishes in a very short

time with very little fat; one can even roast meat and poultry in a wok, but food can also be steamed, fried and simmered. The technique of poaching with the heat turned off gives meat, poultry and fish a remarkable succulence. All these methods have been practised for some 6000 years so it would be surprising if, with such a long history, the Chinese had not arrived at a simple, intelligent and practical cuisine.

The principles of balance in Chinese dietetics are found naturally in the dishes; food is not only essential to life, it can also maintain the harmony of the body, even restore it. It can be a spiritual support, a way of preserving the harmonious interaction of society, of nature and the cosmos.

This is where the fundamental principles of Yin and Yang come in. All foodstuffs come under one or other of these categories. Yin foods are 'cold' – for example, shellfish, vegetables such as cabbage, and certain beans. The Yang foods include fatty meats, oily vegetable matter such as peanuts, and smoked fish. Yin-yang foods, like rice and wheat, are neutral. This system is not unlike the old Western doctrine of 'humours', which served to determine the natural disposition of people and the attributes of natural products.

Whether or not Chinese cuisine is the best in the world, it does rank among those that attach a higher purpose to food, both on a gastronomic level and a philosophical plane. Only in France, Italy and Thailand have I found a similar culture of good eating; it is the traditions of these countries that have most influenced my culinary journey.

In the 1970s, the same period that the general attitude in the United States to food was working towards an increased awareness of natural produce and healthy eating, Europe was converted to Nouvelle Cuisine, of which the principles were as follows: preference given to fresh produce; shorter cooking times; the abandonment of sauces thickened with flour, replacing them with meat juices or vegetables, puréed and whipped up with butter or cream; increasing lightness in dishes and menus; openness to other culinary traditions. Nouvelle Cuisine, as Gault and Millau wrote around this time, did not reject Asian products, condiments or even Asian recipes. Paul Bocuse imported saffron from Iran for his mussel soup; Michel Oliver experimented with Peking duck; Michel Guérard put duck and grapefruit together. Because the need was for fresh, and therefore local, produce, cooks saw themselves obliged to be inventive, forced to find ingenious ways of using available

ingredients. At its best, Nouvelle Cuisine was synonymous with new dishes, new products and new combinations of tastes, everything served as aesthetically as possible.

Nouvelle Cuisine had a liberating influence on my own work and confirmed that my convictions and my methods were well founded. The insistence on fresh, natural produce, precise cooking times, the lightness, colour and freshness in the flavours could not fail to impress me. It reminded me of my Chinese gastronomic education. Of course, Nouvelle Cuisine is now far from new. It was thoroughly tested and sowed the seeds of contemporary cuisine, though some local and traditional dishes have made a comeback on to the scene. Over the course of time it has even become clothed in a new form of classicism, even snobbery, as shown in the over-exploited 'gourmet chic'. But its gains, its combi-

nations, its victories are still real, and I am aware of all that it brought me.

As an American I believe in democracy, including the democracy of good taste. An important underlying theme of my cuisine is the conviction that good eating has nothing to do with social class. It is true that education alone will not change eating habits – especially in the face of the agro-alimentary steamroller, the advertising world and the chemical industries – but one has to start somewhere to make consumers realize that they do have other choices than the ones these forces are attempting to impose on them. And if these other choices are delicious and easy to prepare, so much the better.

My cooking does not pretend to be neo-Californian, neo-Chinese or Franco-American. I am convinced, on the

Occasionally a few Japanese or Mexican elements come to join in the process. I recommend the use of fresh produce, but of course imported products also have a role to play. The important thing to remember is that I am not offering an imitation of Chinese or French or any other cuisine, nor am I attempting to fake them. In exploring their possibilities, widening their potential, I offer them nothing but respect. A recipe, for me, is not a rigid formula. In my opinion cooking is an art, not a science; it feeds on imitation just as much as creation, and more on play than work. So launch yourself into the experience, use your imagination. I know from my own experience that this recreational approach, tinged with passion, produces dishes that are both familiar and exotic and satisfying to the senses.

contrary, that I am carrying on a long tradition. First of all, what is true for French cuisine (according to food writer Richard Olney 'good honest cooking and good French cooking are one and the same thing') is true, in my opinion, for all cooking. After all, American cuisine, while it was for a long time dominated by fairly uncreative German and British traditions, has always been a shifting combination of various different influences. This is increasingly so. Because of this new openness, it too embraces the spirit that motivated Nouvelle Cuisine. My East–West cuisine is just my personal contribution to this same spirit.

Basically, this cuisine deriving from the meeting of East and West is nothing more than the natural and spontaneous combining of ingredients and techniques borrowed principally from China, France, Italy and Thailand.

In each of the recipes that follows I explain what led me to combine the ingredients in this or that manner and why, in my opinion, this particular combination was desirable. I talk about the characteristics of the ingredients, the spices, the herbs and condiments, of the advantages and the limitations of the techniques used, never forgetting to mention any historic, social, even mythological aspects, occasionally adding a few relevant references.

What am I aiming for? I aim to offer you the best of the East and the West and to help you to create new dishes to enjoy. Performing this task has given me immense pleasure.

Ken Hom

Getting the best out of this book

This work is the natural outcome of my multi-cultural experiences and my chosen affinities. The process described here of combining ingredients, condiments and both Asian and Western culinary techniques, is the result of a number of factors: my family origins, my professional life, my journeys and finally my interest in cooking and my great love of food. I learned to cook without recipes; I watched professional cooks at work and followed their instructions, which gave me a certain command of the techniques used, the compatibility of the ingredients, and the simplicity and precise timing, which is the basis of all good cooking. My permanent contact with two cultures opened up possibilities to me of which I took advantage without initially being aware of it. Later, in the course of my extensive travels, I realized that it was this openness that made it so easy for me to adapt to new and unusual ideas. No doubt less encumbered with prejudices than the average person, I adjusted better and had no problem with borrowing methods and customs from other parts of the world. Taste and the appreciation of food is a matter of culture, defined and rooted in the psyche of all mankind, but my adaptability turned out to be a precious gift and a delightful blessing.

So, I learned to cook without the use of recipes. As everyone does. We begin by copying others' techniques, by following instructions and finally, if all goes well, by branching out on our own and creating our own personal cuisine. The important thing, even if the recipes are found in a cookbook, is for cooks to add a little something of themselves to the preparation that makes it worthy of the name cuisine. The recipe is important, of course, but not as important as the care, application and love that one puts into the act of cooking. It is always a very personal act. It is also an ideal way of communing with others by those psychic and sensual routes that form part of the basis of all human interaction, there where the social merges with the biological. It is a question of sharing, of giving and receiving, touching, tasting, smelling and being happy. In a household filled with love and harmony, the simplest of meals will satisfy the senses but, if this spirit of affection and sincerity towards one's fellows is lacking, even the most elaborate of banquets will disappoint.

Recipes represent the letter, but it is the spirit that brings everything to life. All the recipes have been tried and tested by my friends and by me personally. They reflect my culinary preferences. Almost all simple, they rarely if ever require costly ingredients or call for complicated techniques. They are there to initiate you into the preparation of delicious meals but also, more importantly, to help you create your own experience, guided by your imagination. Try these recipes but don't feel imprisoned by them. You are free to modify them according to your taste and your inspiration and, of course, pleasure.

This book is organized in the classic way. You will find some sauces and a minimum of basic stocks. I put emphasis on fish, poultry and meat because it is around these, in my experience, that the most natural and best examples of East meeting West in the kitchen are found. You may perhaps feel that the Asian tastes predominate; this is not my personal impression, except perhaps in the poultry recipes where my mother's culinary heritage is very much in evidence. It is, at any rate, a type of cooking for use every day in the home, traditional and innovative at the same time.

It is there for all to see: these days cooking and food flavours are wide open to new and far-ranging influences. Priority is given to the use of fresh, locally produced ingredients; new cooking techniques are becoming popular; the links between health and diet are becoming more evident; better acceptance is accorded to different types of cuisine from all over the world, which proves that the philosophy and the recipes presented in this book are not so much discoveries as the acceptance of the basic soundness of ancestral culinary practices in Asia. In addition, in this book you will find advice on using new products in the most delicious way possible.

In the 'Menus' section I apply the same principles that underlie my approach to cooking. These menus illustrate the harmonious stylistic unity that I aim for. My theories about cooking have led me to believe that the merging of East with West will produce tasty, nutritious dishes, and these theories are confirmed by my own experience. Now it is up to you to put them to the test and use my experience as a basis on which to build your own. These recipes are for you; don't hesitate to take and use them. Cook with love and enthusiasm and you will discover, as I did, the delights that are in store for you.

Cooking techniques

Grilling

Grilling should be done at a very high temperature with the food basted frequently, so that the outside is seared while the inside remains succulent and moist. Meat, fish, vegetables and even fruit can all be cooked in this way. Larger pieces of meat are best left for about 15 minutes before carving.

Steaming

Steaming is a gentle and delicate method of cooking. The items, placed on a heatproof dish, should be suspended at least 5 cm (2 inches) above boiling water. In this way the food retains all its flavour as well as most of its nutritional value, and never dries out. Several items can be cooked side by side in a basket, as long as there is room for the steam to circulate between them. If too much of the water evaporates add a little more, but do not remove the lid from the steamer unless absolutely necessary.

Sautéing in a wok

When using this specifically Chinese method, all the ingredients must be chopped and ready to hand before beginning to cook them over a fierce heat. From a dietary point of view this is an excellent technique as it is quick, requires little oil and retains the colour, texture and shape of the ingredients. The wok – a utensil specially designed for this type of cooking – is ideal for the purpose.

Frying

Frying in hot oil simultaneously sears the outside of the food and cooks it right through to its centre. The temperature of the oil is all-important: the inside of the food must finish cooking before the outside begins to burn. The Chinese use a wok for frying because it needs much less oil than a normal deep-fat fryer. It is important to check the temperature of the oil before beginning to fry. When it is hot enough a slight haze forms above it. If you drop in a piece of bread or other ingredient, it should sizzle immediately. Bear in mind that the temperature of the oil drops when you add the ingredients, so do not put in more than a few items at a time. Dry them carefully before adding to the oil to avoid spitting, and change the oil as often as possible.

Braising

This is often used for less tender cuts of meat and some vegetables. They must first be browned in fat then simmered for a long time in stock to make them tender and bring out their flavour. Braised dishes freeze very well, so enough for several meals can be prepared at the same time. Any braising stock left over can be also reused; reheating it brings out the flavours.

Roasting

This form of cooking consists of placing the item to be roasted in an oven, where it is surrounded by hot air, which leaves the surface crisp and crunchy while the interior remains tender and succulent. Joints roasted in the oven are best left to rest for 15–20 minutes out of the oven before carving.

Poaching

There is a special Chinese method of poaching; the item to be cooked is briefly immersed in some kind of boiling liquid, then the receptacle is sealed and removed from the heat source. The food remains for a given time in the hot liquid, where it cooks slowly, keeping all its texture, flavour and succulence. Dishes cooked in this manner are very delicate.

Appetizers and salads

Salad with crispy chicken skin and orange and sesame vinaigrette

Fresh tuna salad

Small Chinese ravioli with fresh herbs

Crab and lemon grass quiche

Small steamed shellfish parcels

Duck salad with the flavours of Asia

Nems the way I make them: chicken and tomato rolls

Cubed tomatoes with tarragon and sesame oil

Tomato salad with ginger and chive vinaigrette

Chicken and asparagus salad with sesame

'Hunger is the best aperitif.'

Proverb

'To make a good salad is to be a brilliant diplomatist — the problem is entirely the same in both cases. To know exactly how much oil one must put with one's vinegar.'

Oscar Wilde

Appetizers and salads

In Asia, where meals are not organized into courses, the concept of appetizers or entrées, dishes destined to stimulate the appetite, is quite unknown. These are Western concepts. Dishes equivalent to salads do exist, however, such as marinated dishes or those dressed with vinegar in Japanese cuisine, and marinated or salted vegetables from China. But green salads as eaten in the West have no equivalent in the East. Nevertheless, there are a number of dishes in Asian cooking that could serve as salads and appetizers: Chicken and Tomato Rolls (page 36) are a good example. Likewise, a simple green salad takes on a new meaning when dressed with a Sesame and Orange Vinaigrette (see page 28). All these little dishes demonstrate that, while culinary concepts can differ from one culture to another, flavours know no frontiers.

Salad with crispy chicken skin and
orange and sesame vinaigrette

Serves 2 • **preparation** 3 minutes • **cooking** 6–7 minutes

the skin from
2 chicken breasts
2 tablespoons groundnut
(peanut) oil
2 handfuls young salad leaves
(lettuce, oakleaf lettuce, etc)
2 tablespoons fresh
orange juice
2 tablespoons shallots, finely
chopped and squeezed dry in
kitchen paper (paper towels)
salt and freshly ground
black pepper
1 teaspoon sesame oil

1 Cut the chicken skin into strips 5 cm (2 inches) long and about 6–7 mm (¼ inch) wide. Heat a small frying pan and add 1 tablespoon groundnut oil. When it is hot add the strips of chicken skin and fry them slowly until crisp. Remove from the fat and drain them on kitchen paper.

2 Wash and dry the salad. In a bowl, mix together the orange juice, chopped shallot, salt and pepper. Whisk gently as you add the sesame oil and the rest of the groundnut oil. Add the salad leaves and mix carefully. Garnish with the strips of chicken skin and serve.

In this recipe, I sought to bring out the freshness of the garden salad by using a delicate dressing made with orange juice, which is less acidic than vinegar. The sesame and groundnut oils complement each other without overshadowing either the liveliness of the orange or the subtle sweetness of the lettuce. The slowly fried and lightly salted strips of chicken skin give texture and flavour to the salad. It could not be simpler, and the quantities can easily be doubled or trebled according to your need.

Fresh tuna salad

Serves 4 • **preparation** 20 minutes • **cooking** 10 minutes

225 g (8 oz) raw tuna fillet
1 tablespoon light soy sauce
1 tablespoon lime juice
½ red onion, peeled and very finely sliced
1 tablespoon Japanese rice wine vinegar
1 tablespoon finely chopped fresh coriander (cilantro)
120 ml (½ cup) Tomato Concassé (page 221)
1 tablespoon sesame oil
1 large ripe avocado peeled and sliced

1 Cut the tuna into thin slices across the grain.

2 In a bowl, mix the tuna with the soy sauce and lime juice. Leave to marinate for 20 minutes. In a separate bowl, mix the onion, vinegar and coriander. Leave to macerate for 10 minutes then mix in the sesame oil and Tomato Concassé.

3 Arrange the tuna, onion and tomato mixture and the slices of avocado side by side on individual plates.

For me, the freshness of the fish, the subtlety of the flavours and the smell of the sea sum up Japanese cooking. The influence it has exerted on Western cooking strikes me as profound and very beneficial. This influence appears – among other things – in the presentation of dishes, where eye-appeal is as important as flavour. I like the simplicity of Japanese cooking as opposed to the baroque profusion of Chinese cuisine. In this recipe, the Asian ingredients (raw tuna, rice wine, soy sauce) mixed with the Western ingredients (avocado, tomato) are presented in an almost Japanese manner. This unusual but easy to make salad is as pretty as it is fresh and light.

Small Chinese ravioli
with fresh herbs

Makes about 60 ravioli • **preparation** 30 minutes • **cooking** 20–25 minutes

450 g (1 lb) minced (ground) pork
1 teaspoon finely chopped fresh rosemary
1 tablespoon finely chopped fresh thyme
1 tablespoon finely chopped fresh marjoram
1 tablespoon finely chopped fresh coriander (cilantro)
1 tablespoon finely chopped chives
2 tablespoons finely chopped spring onions (scallions)
1 tablespoon light soy sauce
1 tablespoon Shaoxing rice wine
1 packet (package) rice sheets for Chinese ravioli
Tomato-ginger sauce (page 222)
freshly grated Parmesan cheese

1 In a mixing bowl, mix the minced pork with the herbs, spring onions, soy sauce and rice wine.

2 Place 1 small tablespoonful of the filling in the centre of each square of pastry, gather up the 4 corners and pinch them firmly together. Continue until all the filling is used up.

3 Place a wire grid or bamboo basket in a wok, or use a steamer. Pour 5 cm (2 inches) water into the receptacle and bring it to the boil. Lay the ravioli on a heatproof plate, place this on the grid or in the upper part of the steamer, cover and cook for 20–25 minutes. Serve with the Tomato-ginger sauce and grated Parmesan.

We all have childhood memories of favourite dishes the aroma of which brings back happy memories. For me, it is steamed ravioli. This form of cooking preserves the most delicate flavours and textures. I used this traditional Chinese method to bring together typical Asian tastes — soy sauce and rice wine — with strongly flavoured herbs currently used in the West. The mixture of flavours that results gives a tasty little parcel, traditional and completely new at the same time.

Crab and
lemon grass quiche

Makes 1 quiche • **preparation** 30 minutes • **cooking** 20–25 minutes

Pastry (pie dough)
60 g (4½ tablespoons) softened butter
½ teaspoon salt
120 g (¾ cup) flour
2 tablespoons iced water
2 tablespoons single (light) cream

Quiche filling
3 eggs
250 ml (generous 1 cup) single cream
salt and freshly ground black pepper
1 teaspoon finely chopped fresh root ginger
2 tablespoons finely chopped lemon grass
3 tablespoons freshly grated Parmesan cheese
1 tablespoon finely chopped spring onion (scallion)
2 teaspoons finely chopped chives
200 g (7 oz) fresh crabmeat

1 In a mixing bowl, rub the butter and salt into the flour with your fingertips to obtain a fine sandy consistency. Add the iced water and the single cream and work lightly for a few moments then roll it into a ball on a floured surface. Wrap the dough in clingfilm (plastic wrap) and store in the refrigerator for 30 minutes.

2 Preheat the oven to 180°C (350°F, Gas Mark 4). Roll out the dough to a depth of 2.5 cm (1 inch). Place it in the centre of a tart mould (mold) and stretch it out with the fingers until it covers the inside of the mould. Cover the base with foil and weight it with 300 g (1¾ cups) dried beans to prevent it from rising while cooking. Bake in the oven for 12 minutes.

3 Remove the beans and foil and prick the base of the tart all over with a fork then let it cook for a further 10 minutes. Remove from the oven and leave to cool.

4 Mix all the ingredients for the filling together and pour into the pastry case (shell). Sprinkle the Parmesan over the top and increase the oven temperature to 200°C (400°F, Gas Mark 6). Cook for 25 minutes, or until the filling has set.

Quiche was one of the great discoveries I made when I was exploring French popular cuisine. It has rather gone out of fashion but I still hold it in high esteem because it lends itself to such an infinite range of delicious variations. Here, for example, I use it to mix three flavours adored in Asia — those of fresh crab, ginger and lemon grass. The two aromatic substances bring out the best in the delicate flavour of the crab. A slim-line version of the family quiche.

Small steamed
shellfish parcels

Makes 18 parcels • **preparation** 15 minutes • **cooking** 8–10 minutes

225 g (8 oz) large raw prawns (shrimp), thawed
225 g (8 oz) fresh scallops without the coral, cut into 18 slices (about 6 scallops)
1 packet (package) Vietnamese rice pastry sheets (banh trang) about 22 cm (8½ inches) in diameter
grated zest of 1 lemon
18 strips fresh red chilli
18 fresh basil leaves
Tomato-ginger sauce (page 222)

Marinade
2 tablespoons fresh lemon juice
1 tablespoon Shaoxing rice wine or dry sherry
1 tablespoon light soy sauce
salt and freshly ground black pepper
¼ teaspoon ground cumin

1 In a bowl, mix the ingredients together for the marinade. Add the prawns, peeled (shelled) and cut in half lengthways, and the scallops. Cover and leave to marinate in the refrigerator for 1 hour.

2 Fill a mixing bowl with warm water and soak each of the rice sheets for a few seconds to soften them, then drain them and dry them on kitchen paper (paper towels). Drain the prawns and scallops and pat them dry on kitchen paper.

3 At the centre of each pastry sheet place, in this order: 1 pinch of lemon zest, 1 strip of chilli, 1 slice of scallop, 1 basil leaf and finally, 1 half prawn.

4 Fold the pastry in the form of an envelope in the following manner: fold the lower part of the sheet (the one nearest to you) over the filling to two thirds of the depth of the sheet. Fold in the left and right sides to meet in the centre. Push the filling halfway to the top edge then fold this edge back over the parcel, tucking the end of the sheet under to hold it firm. Carry on until all the filling is used.

5 Pour 5 cm (2 inches) of water into a wok fitted with a steamer basket or a grid, or into the base of a steamer. Place the parcels on a heatproof plate in the basket and steam for 8–10 minutes. Serve immediately with Tomato-ginger sauce if liked (page 222).

For this recipe I borrowed the Chinese technique for cooking dim sum *by steaming them in a greaseproof (waxed) paper envelope, replacing the paper with the Vietnamese thin rice pastry. When cooked, these little parcels become transparent, allowing their delicious contents to show through. And since the rice pastry is edible there is no need to remove the envelope, which is eaten with the rest. Once the parcels are made, steaming them takes only a few minutes. The basil can be replaced by other fresh herbs.*

Duck salad
with the flavours of Asia

Serves 4 • **preparation** 15 minutes

400 g (14 oz) cooked duck
with fat removed

2 heads chicory, cleaned
and trimmed

2 mangoes, peeled and sliced

Vinaigrette

1 tablespoon finely chopped garlic

1 tablespoon finely chopped
shallot, squeezed dry in
kitchen paper (paper towels)

2 tablespoons spring onions
(scallions), finely chopped

salt and freshly ground
black pepper

2 teaspoons sesame oil

2 teaspoons spicy soy sauce

1 teaspoon light soy sauce

3 tablespoons finely chopped
chives

1 Break up the duck meat (the equivalent of half a roast duck or Peking duck) into slivers and set them aside. Mix all the ingredients for the vinaigrette together and pour it over the duck. Mix well.

2 Break the leaves from the chicory and place a layer of them on individual plates, cover with the duck salad and garnish with slices of mango. Serve immediately.

I have long appreciated duck cooked in the Chinese way – braised, roasted or steamed. But France was where I discovered duck salad. It's an excellent way of serving this rich and tasty meat, and also of using up leftovers. In this recipe the cold duck is dressed with an uncompromisingly Asian vinaigrette, chicory and mangoes. These ingredients go well together and balance the pronounced flavour of the duck. Use either a duck you have roasted yourself, confit of duck or Peking duck. Once you have tried this recipe you will undoubtedly want to make it again.

Nems the way I make them:
chicken and tomato rolls

Makes 35–40 rolls • **preparation** 60 minutes • **cooking** 20 minutes

60 g (2¼ oz) soya vermicelli

225 g (8 oz) chicken breast cut into fine strips about 7.5 cm (3 inches) long

salt and freshly ground black pepper

2 tablespoons olive oil

1 tablespoon finely chopped spring onions (scallions)

2 tablespoons finely chopped chives

2 teaspoons finely chopped fresh coriander (cilantro)

2 tablespoons finely chopped sun-dried tomatoes

1 packet (package) Vietnamese rice sheets (*banh trang*) about 22 cm (8½ inches) in diameter

300 ml (1¼ cups) groundnut (peanut) oil

To seal the rolls

3 tablespoons flour

3 tablespoons water

1 Soak the soya vermicelli in warm water for 15 minutes. Drain them in a sieve (strainer) and cut them into three along the length then dry them in a cloth.

2 Meanwhile, in a large bowl mix the strips of chicken, salt and pepper, olive oil, spring onions, chives, coriander and sun-dried tomatoes. Add the vermicelli and mix well. This can be done in advance.

3 Prepare the 'glue' by mixing the flour and water together. When you are ready to make your 'nems,' fill a large bowl with warm water. Drop a rice sheet into it and leave to soften for 1 minute. Remove and dry on a cloth. Place a large tablespoon of the filling on a sheet and roll it up, tucking in the ends. Roll it on the work surface to obtain a regular cylindrical shape.

4 Glue the edge of the sheet with the flour and water mix; you should have a firm, tight roll about 7.5 cm (3 inches) long. Lay it on a plate and continue until all the filling is used. (The rolls can be prepared in advance up to this stage. Wrap them in a clean cloth but not too tightly.)

5 Heat a wok (or a sauté pan) over a high heat until it is very hot, then pour in the oil. When it begins to smoke reduce the heat to medium and fry the rolls until nicely browned. At the start they tend to stick to each other so don't cook more than a few at a time. If they should stick together don't try and separate them until you have taken them out of the oil. Drain them on kitchen paper (paper towels) and serve immediately.

The wrappings for the Vietnamese 'nems' are made from rice, unlike Chinese spring rolls, which are made from wheat. I find the Vietnamese version has a more interesting flavour and texture than the Chinese one: lighter, crisper, more appropriate for this recipe, which mixes chicken, herbs, dried tomatoes and soya vermicelli.

Cubed tomatoes with
tarragon and sesame oil

Serves 4 • **preparation** 5 minutes

750 g (1 lb 10 oz) well-ripened
fresh tomatoes
2 teaspoons fresh tarragon leaves
2 tablespoons finely
chopped chives

Vinaigrette
1 tablespoon lemon juice
2 teaspoons Dijon mustard
1 teaspoon sugar
salt and freshly ground
black pepper
1 tablespoon sesame oil

1 Blanch the tomatoes for 10 seconds then peel and de-seed them. Cut the flesh into 3.5 cm (1 ⅓ inch) cubes and place them in a sieve (strainer) to drain. Meanwhile, mix all the ingredients for the vinaigrette together in a bowl.

2 Shortly before serving, add the tarragon and chives to the cubes of tomato, pour on the vinaigrette, mix and serve immediately.

This simple and delicious salad is best served in the tomato season. The fresh French herbs go well with the nutty, Asian flavour of toasted sesame oil. All the ingredients are easily found, but it is important that the sauce is only added just before serving.

Tomato salad with ginger and chive vinaigrette

Serves 4 • **preparation** 5 minutes

500 g (1 lb 2 oz) cherry tomatoes, red or yellow

Vinaigrette
1 tablespoon finely chopped shallot
2 tablespoons finely chopped chives
1 tablespoon finely chopped fresh root ginger
2 tablespoons lemon juice
2 teaspoons Dijon mustard
salt and freshly ground black pepper
4 tablespoons extra virgin olive oil

1 Halve the tomatoes. Wrap the chopped shallot and chives in a cloth and squeeze out the excess moisture.

2 Add the shallot and chives to the other ingredients of the vinaigrette and mix well. Pour the vinaigrette over the tomatoes and serve immediately.

Ginger and chives — a typically Asiatic duo — come together in this French tomato salad to give it a piquant and original touch. Once again it is an easy recipe. What is more it is refreshing and full of flavour.

Chicken and asparagus salad
with sesame paste dressing

Serves 4 • **preparation** 15 minutes • **cooking** 5 minutes

225 g (8 oz) green asparagus
450 g (1 lb) chicken breast, cut into strips 6–7 mm (¼ inch) thick and about 7.5 cm (3 inches) long

Vinaigrette
1 egg yolk
2 teaspoons Dijon mustard
salt and freshly ground black pepper
2 teaspoons finely chopped garlic
2 teaspoons sesame paste
120 ml (½ cup) extra virgin olive oil
3 tablespoons finely chopped shallots, squeezed of their juice
1 handful fresh basil
3 tablespoons finely chopped chives
2 sweet red peppers preserved in vinegar, cut into strips

1 Bring a saucepan of water to the boil and prepare a bowl with cold water and ice. Blanch the asparagus (washed, peeled and cut on a slight bias into 5 cm (2 inch) lengths) for a few moments. As soon as the water returns to the boil, lift them out with a slotted spoon and drop them into the iced water. Remove the pan from the heat and drop in the chicken pieces. Cover and leave to cook in the residual heat for 4 minutes. Drain and set aside.

2 For the vinaigrette, beat the egg yolk, mustard, salt and pepper together in a small bowl. Add the garlic and sesame paste and mix thoroughly. Drizzle in the oil in a thin, continuous stream, beating constantly until it is incorporated.

3 Place the chicken, asparagus, shallots and vinaigrette in a salad bowl and mix together. Add the basil and chives and mix again. Garnish with the strips of red pepper and serve.

In many Asian regions cold chicken salad dressed with sesame vinaigrette is a very prestigious dish. Asparagus, however, is of Western origin. It has nonetheless been enthusiastically adopted in eastern Asia. Chinese cooks, for the most part, sauté it in a wok but I find it just as delicious simply blanched and served with a spicy vinaigrette. This one is a variation of a French vinaigrette with an added touch of sesame paste. It is easy to make and excellent in the spring and when the weather is hot.

Soups

Courgette and ginger soup

Chinese pear and watercress soup

Oxtail soup

Soup with goat's cheese *wonton*

Cold tomato and lemon grass soup

Oyster consommé

Cream of asparagus with coriander

Scallop soup with sweetcorn and ginger

Cream of sweetcorn, lemon grass and ginger, served with chilli bean paste

'Between soup and love, the first is the best.'

Proverb

Venite ad me omnes qui stomacho laboratis et ego restaurabo.
('Come to me, you whose stomachs cry out from hunger and I will heal you.')
A sign on Monsieur Boulanger's inexpensive, popular restaurant, opened in the eighteenth century in Paris, and which was one of the first restaurants recorded in French history.

Soups

Soups are just as popular in Asia as they are in Europe, but their status and the part they play differ from one culture to another. In some parts of Asia they can be virtually non-existent, as in India, or taken as a drink, as in Japan. In China soup is neither an entrée nor a preliminary course but an integral part of the meal. Served in a large soup tureen in the centre of the table, surrounded by all the other dishes, it is consumed throughout the meal, either as a 'refresher' between dishes or as a drink to accompany them. Indeed, water is never served with a Chinese meal; as to tea, that is served before and after, but never during a meal.

In the West, soup is an entrée, an appetizer, sometimes even a complete meal, but never, as in China, an accompaniment or support. In the following recipes I have borrowed formulas from different culinary traditions and added new seasonings to them to bring out the familiar flavours and give them an extra dimension. An example of this is the Cream of Sweetcorn with Lemon Grass and Ginger, served with Chilli Bean Paste, (page 54) or the Soup with Goat's Cheese *wonton* (page 48) flavoured with saffron, chives and coriander (cilantro).

I have also included a cold soup, something practically unknown in Asia, although in China a cold, sweet soup is sometimes served in the course of a banquet. I have, therefore, included one of these in the chapter on desserts (p 201). In the West, where soups are a separate culinary category, cold soups have a respected place on the menu.

But whether in East or West, never forget that good soup cannot be made without a good stock.

Courgette and
ginger soup

Serves 4–6 • **preparation** 45 minutes • **cooking** 10 minutes

900 g (2 lb) courgettes (zucchini), peeled and cut into julienne strips

1 tablespoon coarse salt

2 tablespoons extra virgin olive oil

1 finely chopped small onion

4 spring onions (scallions), finely chopped

3 tablespoons finely chopped shallot

1 tablespoon finely chopped fresh root ginger

1 tablespoon sugar

1 litre (4 cups) Chicken Stock (page 218)

2 tablespoons crème fraîche (or sour cream)

salt and freshly ground black pepper

a few purple chive flowers or some chopped chives, to garnish (optional)

1 Place the strips of courgette in a stainless steel or enamel sieve (strainer), add the coarse salt and mix well. Leave to drain for 30–45 minutes then rinse them, wrap in a cloth and squeeze out as much moisture as possible. Set aside.

2 Heat the olive oil in a large sauté pan. Soften the onion, spring onion, shallot and ginger over a low heat for about 5 minutes without letting them colour. Add the courgettes and sugar and mix well.

3 Meanwhile, bring the Chicken Stock to the boil in a separate pan. Sweat the courgettes for a few more minutes then add the hot stock and remove from the heat. Using a ladle, add small quantities at a time to a blender or food processor and process to a smooth cream-like consistency. Pour the mixture into a large stainless steel bowl and leave to cool. To speed up the cooling, place the bowl into iced water.

4 When the soup is almost cold, gently stir in the crème fraîche. Adjust the seasoning. Store the soup in the refrigerator until needed. Garnish with the chive flowers or chopped chives if you like.

I first tasted this soup at the Gaddi restaurant of the Peninsula hotel in Hong Kong. I decided to re-create the recipe with a few added touches of my own. This very simple soup makes an excellent introduction to all kinds of meals. You could follow it with a roast, such as Roast Pork with Chinese Spices (page 128).

Chinese pear and
watercress soup

Serves 4–6 • **preparation** 5 minutes • **cooking** 5 minutes

750 g (1 lb 10 oz) *nashi* (Chinese pears), peeled and de-pipped
1 large bunch watercress, picked over and washed
1 litre (4 cups) Chicken Stock (page 218)
2 tablespoons butter
2 tablespoons crème fraîche (or sour cream)
2 teaspoons sugar
salt and freshly ground black pepper

1 Cut the pears into quarters and set aside. Dry the watercress on kitchen paper (paper towels).

2 Bring the Chicken Stock to simmering point in a saucepan. Add the pear quarters and cook over a medium heat for about 5 minutes. Remove from the heat, add the watercress and leave to cool. When the soup is tepid process it, a little at a time, in a blender to a smooth cream-like consistency.

3 Return the mixture to the saucepan, add the butter, crème fraîche and sugar and season with salt and pepper. Bring back to a simmer and cook for a further 5 minutes without allowing it to boil. This soup can be served hot or cold.

This is my version of a soup my mother used to make for me as a child. Her recipe was strictly Chinese and very simple. As to me, I have added a few Western touches — the cream and the butter — in order to achieve a richer result. Reducing the soup to a purée is also a Western concept; Asians prefer contrasting textures. I do feel that this method is valid here.

The pears used here are nashi, *an Asian variety known in France, UK and USA as 'Japanese pears' or 'Chinese pears.' They are also called 'pear-apples' because, when ripe, they have the flavour of the best kind of pears but retain the crisp texture of apples. If you are unable to find them, use ripe but firm pears.*

Oxtail soup

Serves 4–6 • **preparation** 15 minutes • **cooking** 1 hour 40 minutes

2 kg (4 lb 8 oz) oxtail, cut into short lengths

1 litre (4 cups) Chicken Stock (page 218)

250 ml (generous 1 cup) Shaoxing rice wine or dry sherry

100 g (3½ oz) spring onions (scallions), chopped

2 tablespoons light soy sauce

5 tablespoons capers, drained

2 tablespoons finely chopped garlic

3 tablespoons Dijon mustard

1 tablespoon sesame oil

1 Blanch the pieces of oxtail in boiling water for 10 minutes. Drain off all the water then place the oxtail pieces in a large casserole, add the Chicken Stock, rice wine and soy sauce. Bring to simmering point, cover and cook over a low heat for 1½ hours, or until the meat is tender. Remove the oxtail pieces and keep them warm in a dish.

2 Mix the spring onions, capers, garlic, mustard and sesame oil together and pour over the meat. Serve the consommé in bowls and the meat separately.

Oxtail soup forms part of several Asian traditions. When I was a child it appeared frequently on the table, not only because it was cheap but also because we loved nibbling the tasty meat lurking in the crevices of the bones. Oxtail does indeed have a rich flavour, which I learned to appreciate very early. We drank the soup first then we dunked the pieces of oxtail in a mixture of soy sauce, ginger and chopped chives. Here I have maintained the traditional Chinese recipe, but have added a few European condiments, which, in my opinion, improve this venerable dish even further: mustard, capers and garlic. The rice wine adds an aromatic touch to this solid, comforting soup — a real treat in winter.

Soup with
goat's cheese *wonton*

Serves 4–6 • **preparation** 15 minutes • **cooking** 5 minutes

1 packet (package) pastry sheets for *wonton* (Chinese ravioli)
2 litres (8½ cups) Chicken Stock (page 218)
2 litres (8½ cups) water
2 teaspoons salt
chopped chives, to garnish

Filling
125 g (4½ oz) mild goat's cheese
125 g (4½ oz) ricotta cheese
2 tablespoons finely chopped chives
3 tablespoons finely chopped spring onions (scallions)
1 tablespoon finely chopped fresh coriander (cilantro)
salt and freshly ground black pepper

1 For the filling: mix the 2 cheeses, chives, spring onions, coriander and salt and pepper together in a bowl with a wooden spatula.

2 Place 2 teaspoons of the filling in the centre of each square of *wonton* pastry. Lift the borders of the pastry and pinch them to knit them together. The humidity present in the filling should suffice to seal them, but be careful not to puncture the pastry. Lay these *wonton* on a floured surface as you complete them.

3 Bring the stock to the boil in a pan and season with salt if necessary. In another pan bring the 2 litres (8½ cups) of water to the boil and add the salt. Drop the *wonton* in for 30 seconds. When they come back to the surface lift them out carefully with a slotted spoon and transfer them to the simmering stock. Cook them for 2–3 minutes. You may have to do this in several batches.

4 Pour the soup into a soup tureen, or individual bowls, garnish with the chopped chives and serve immediately.

All ravioli are born equal, but some are more equal than others. I think, for example, that the Chinese way, consisting of serving the ravioli (or wonton) in a rich, light consommé, shows them to best advantage. And here, instead of the traditional minced (ground) pork filling, I have used the marvellous, earthy flavour of mild goat's cheese, which goes perfectly with chives and coriander. This recipe is a good illustration of the strong points of both styles of cooking, Asian and European. With the wonton *sheets that you can find in any Asian grocery stores this soup is ready in just a few minutes,*

Cold tomato and
lemon grass soup

Serves 4 • **preparation** 20 minutes • **cooking** 10 minutes

20 g (1½ tablespoons) butter

2 tablespoons extra virgin olive oil

1 large onion, finely chopped

3 stems of lemon grass, finely chopped

500 ml (2 cups) Chicken Stock (page 218)

750 ml (3 cups) Tomato Concassé (page 221)

salt and freshly ground black pepper

2 tablespoons sugar

2 tablespoons single (light) cream

To garnish

2 tablespoons finely chopped chives

1 tablespoon finely chopped fresh coriander (cilantro)

1 In a saucepan, heat the butter and olive oil then add the onion and the lemon grass. Leave to sweat over a low heat for 5 minutes. Add the Chicken Stock and Tomato Concassé and mix well. Add salt and pepper and the sugar. Cook over a low heat for 5 minutes then leave to cool. Process in a blender – in small quantities if necessary.

2 Leave the soup to cool completely. Cover with clingfilm (plastic wrap) and store in the refrigerator. Just before serving, incorporate the cream and garnish with chives and coriander.

It is only a short time ago – a little more than one century – since tomatoes were introduced into the venerable Chinese cuisine. Nevertheless, they are now universally popular. East and West really do meet, whatever one says. Here I have mixed the European tomato soup with a herb that is purely Asian – lemon grass. Its strong and yet subtle aroma offers an agreeable contrast to the rich, smooth tomato soup without the need to add a touch of acidity such as lemon juice. This makes a very good summer dish, as well as an excellent entrée, but it can also form the basis of a light meal. It can be prepared in advance and stored in the refrigerator as it keeps its flavour well. It can also, of course, be served hot.

Oyster consommé

Serves 4 • **preparation** 15 minutes • **cooking** 5 minutes

500 ml (2 cups) Fish Stock
(page 219)
12 fresh oysters
250 ml (generous 1 cup) Tomato
Concassé (page 221)
1 teaspoon fresh root ginger
1 tablespoon light soy sauce
1 tablespoon Shaoxing rice
wine or dry sherry
2 tablespoons fresh coriander
(cilantro) sprigs, to garnish

1 Bring the Fish Stock to the boil in a saucepan.

2 Add the oysters minus their shells but with their juices, the Tomato Concassé, the ginger, finely chopped, soy sauce and rice wine. Cook over a very low heat for 5 minutes and garnish with the coriander sprigs just before serving.

Among the many Chinese and Japanese soups, my favourites are the clear, light ones, each with its own subtle aromas. The simplest ones are the best, made with fresh ingredients that have undergone as little change as possible. I applied this rule to my oyster consommé. China and Japan are renowned for their seafood cookery and oysters are the very essence of the sea. This consommé is, therefore, purely Asian in concept, though the flavours are familiar to the Western palate. I use ginger to balance the natural richness of the oysters and to lightly flavour the consommé. This is a quick and easy soup to make and an elegant start to a meal.

Cream of asparagus
with coriander

Serves 4 • **preparation** 5 minutes • **cooking** 5 minutes

1 litre (4 cups) Chicken Stock
(page 218)

450 g (1 lb) green asparagus

salt and freshly ground
black pepper

2 tablespoons finely chopped
spring onion (scallion)

2 tablespoons finely
chopped shallot

1 tablespoon butter

3 tablespoons crème fraîche
(or sour cream)

2 tablespoons finely chopped
fresh coriander (cilantro)

1 Pour the Chicken Stock into a saucepan, add the asparagus, cut into 5 cm (2 inches) lengths and cook for 2–3 minutes. Leave to cool then blend in a food processor. Season with salt and pepper to taste.

2 Pour the mixture back into the saucepan and, over a very low heat, add the spring onion, shallot, butter, crème fraîche and coriander. Simmer over a low heat for 1 minute then serve immediately.

Asparagus in season is so delicious it is pointless to add anything to it. In this soup the vegetable should be presented with all its qualities of flavour, colour and texture. I have therefore prepared it in the simplest possible way. The crème fraîche gives it a touch of sweetness, whereas the coriander, a very popular garnish for soups in southern China and Thailand, brings a touch of earthiness, which harmonizes perfectly with the exquisite flavour of green asparagus. This soup will enchant your guests.

Scallop soup with
sweetcorn and ginger

Serves 6–8 • **preparation** 10 minutes • **cooking** 5 minutes

1 litre (4 cups) fish Stock
(page 219)

450 g (1 lb) cleaned fresh scallops
without the coral

300 g (10½ oz) fresh sweetcorn
(corn) cut from the cob (ear),
about 3 fresh cobs

2 tablespoons Shaoxing rice
wine or dry sherry

1 tablespoon finely chopped
fresh root ginger

3 tablespoons finely chopped
spring onion (scallion)

1 tablespoon sugar

salt and freshly ground
black pepper

2 tablespoons single (light) cream

20 g (1½ tablespoons) butter

3 tablespoons finely chopped
chives, to garnish

1 Bring the Fish Stock to the boil in a saucepan and add the scallops and sweetcorn. Cook over a low heat for 2 minutes, without boiling. Add the rice wine, ginger, spring onion, sugar, salt and pepper and leave to simmer for a further 1 minute, then cool for a few minutes and process in a blender.

2 Pour the mixture back into the saucepan and bring back to simmering point. Adjust the seasoning then add the cream and butter, mixing carefully. Divide it between individual bowls or serve in a soup tureen, garnished with chives.

This combination of classic flavours, textures and aromas of East and West is lifted and harmonized by the ginger, which links the two hemispheres. In Asia, chicken stock would be used instead of fish stock and the ingredients would not be blended. However, I find that the result, in this case, is superior. This very simple to prepare soup needs to be reheated over very low heat and would be marvellous at the start of a meal.

Cream of sweetcorn, lemon grass and ginger, served with chilli bean paste

Serves 4–6 • **preparation** 15 minutes • **cooking** 15 minutes

2 tablespoons extra virgin olive oil

1 tablespoon finely chopped fresh root ginger

2 tablespoons lemon grass bulb, finely chopped

2 tablespoons finely chopped shallot

1 small onion, finely chopped

300 g (10½ oz) fresh sweetcorn cut from the cob (ear) with a sharp knife, about 3 cobs

1 litre (4 cups) Chicken Stock (page 218)

salt and freshly ground black pepper

2 teaspoons sugar

2 tablespoons single (light) cream

2 teaspoons chilli (chili) bean paste (or less, according to taste), to garnish

fresh coriander (cilantro) sprigs, to garnish

1 Heat the olive oil in a saucepan. Add the ginger, lemon grass, shallot and onion and sweat them over a low heat for 2 minutes. Add the sweetcorn and cook for a further 1 minute. Add the Chicken Stock and bring to simmering point. Cook over a low heat for a further 5 minutes then season with salt and pepper and add the sugar and cream. Remove from the heat and leave to cool at room temperature.

2 Process the soup a little at a time in a blender, pulsing the motor for 2–3 minutes at a time. Return the soup to the saucepan and bring back to a simmer.

3 If you serve it in a tureen, add the chilli bean paste in the centre of the soup and stir carefully so as to create a spiral motif. If in individual bowls, place ¼ teaspoon chilli bean paste in the centre of each bowl and stir in the same way, or mix in completely. You could also leave your guests to garnish their own soup. Garnish with coriander sprigs.

Sweetcorn is far from unknown in modern Asia, but it remains an ingredient of Western origin. Here I have interpreted one of America's favourite recipes — cream of fresh sweetcorn — and doubled the pleasure with the addition of some of my favourite Asian flavours: lemon grass, ginger and chilli bean paste. If you like spicy flavours, the taste and appearance of this soup will delight you. If you can't find fresh sweetcorn, don't use the canned variety; young courgettes (zucchini) would make a good substitute.

Fish and shellfish

Grilled crab and lobster

Steamed scallops

Steamed fish with tomatoes and basil

Fillets of fish poached with ginger

'Crystal' prawns with basil, peppers and garlic

A whole fish fried crisp with tomatoes

Mussels with lemon grass butter

Salmon fillet with ginger, basil, tomato and fine salt

A whole fish in a papillote with the flavours of Asia

Spicy prawns stewed with ginger

Abalone sautéed with broccoli

Salmon wrapped in Chinese cabbage leaves and steamed

Fish steamed with spring onions and garlic shoots

Prawns sautéed with mustard and coriander

Crab pancakes with Asian spices

Fish soup flavoured with ginger

Sautéed prawns with carrots and asparagus

Scallops with three kinds of mushrooms

Jade prawns with flat-leaf parsley, coriander and basil

Shellfish, butter sauce and black beans

Fish

Seafood is appreciated the world over, but in China, and especially in Japan, it is of primary importance. For thousands of years the Japanese have lived on what their fishermen took from the sea, and their cuisine is based on the variety and freshness of the fish and shellfish.

China, too, with its abundant rivers and long coastline, gives fish pride of place. When it comes to the rich potential of food from the sea, Asian cooks have nothing to learn from Western chefs, and all are well aware of the important role that the freshness of the raw ingredients plays in the success of a dish. No cook, however able, could prepare an acceptable dish using fish that was less than perfectly fresh. In many parts of Asia, a fish that has ceased to wriggle is no longer considered fit to eat. In Hong Kong, restaurants display big tanks where the fish continue to swim until the very moment they are taken out and prepared for the table. It's a costly method, but well worth the price. It is impossible to argue about the freshness of the fish. In the Hong Kong markets, fish are filleted while still alive – 'with their hearts still beating,' as the locals say.

Shellfish

Prawns (shrimp), langoustines, crayfish, crab, lobster, scallops, abalone and other shellfish are equally popular in both East and West. I have concentrated on using those methods of cooking that bring out their flavour, which is delicate and pronounced at the same time. Indeed, while it is always important to cook to the best of one's ability, it is the fragile and delicate shellfish that require the most careful handling. This is why the best methods of cooking them are steaming, poaching and frying. While lobster and crayfish are expensive and tend to be kept for special occasions, when they are in season crabs are relatively cheap and every region of the world has its own delicious varieties. The golden rule is to buy only perfectly fresh, preferably live, shellfish. Once they are dead they lose much of their flavour. Which is why many Chinese refuse to buy or eat them if they are already cooked.

Grilled crab
and lobster

Serves 4–6 • **preparation** 15 minutes • **cooking** 15 minutes

2 live crabs or spider
crabs about 450–700 g
(1–1 lb 9 oz) each

2 live lobsters about
450–500 g (1–1 lb 2 oz) each

3 tablespoons extra virgin
olive oil

1 tablespoon sesame oil

1 Leave the shellfish in the refrigerator for 1 hour to put them to sleep. Mix both oils together. With a cleaver or a large knife, cut the crabs and lobsters in half along their length. Remove the gills, the mandibles and the eyes, also the intestines. Leave intact the crabs' creamy yellow liver parts and the greenish ones of the lobsters. Lightly brush all the surfaces with the oil mixture and set aside.

2 Light the barbecue. When the embers have turned whitish, grill the crabs and lobsters. They are ready the moment the shells have turned red and the flesh is firm but still translucent. Serve immediately.

Both crabs and lobsters have a fine, delicate flavour. There is nothing like cooking them on a barbecue to preserve this. Steaming shellfish in the shell retains all the natural flavours and creaminess of the flesh. Serve these grilled shellfish with Mayonnaise Flavoured with Ginger and Chives *(page 223).*

Steamed scallops

Serves 4–6 • **preparation** 20 minutes • **cooking** 5–8 minutes

700 g (1 lb 9 oz) fresh scallops without roe, cleaned and trimmed and left whole
2 teaspoons Chinese salt with Sichuan pepper (glossary, page 237)
1 teaspoon orange zest, cut into fine julienne strips
1 tablespoon Shaoxing rice wine or dry sherry
freshly ground black pepper
4 tablespoons cold butter, cut into small pieces
3 tablespoons finely chopped spring onion (scallion)

1 In a large bowl, mix together the scallops, spiced salt, orange zest, rice wine and black pepper to taste. Leave to marinate for 15 minutes.

2 Transfer the scallops, with their marinade, into a heatproof bowl and place this in a steamer basket in a wok, or in the upper part of a steamer. Steam gently for 5–8 minutes.

3 Remove the bowl from the basket, drain and set the scallops aside, retaining the cooking juices. Reduce these juices by half in a saucepan. Gradually incorporate the butter, a little at a time, whisking constantly, then stir in the chopped spring onion. Serve the scallops coated in this sauce.

Nothing is better than the gentle, moist heat of steam for preserving the soft, subtle flavour of scallops.

Steamed fish with tomatoes and basil

Serves 4 • **preparation** 12 minutes • **cooking** 15 minutes

1 whole firm-fleshed fish
(sole, turbot, brill, bass, etc.)
about 1.25 kg (2 lb 12 oz), gutted,
trimmed and, if necessary, scaled
1 tablespoon coarse salt
freshly ground white pepper
1 handful fresh basil leaves
leaves and stems of a bulb of
fennel, coarsely chopped
250 ml (generous 1 cup) Tomato
Concassé (page 221)
1 tablespoon finely chopped
shallot
75 g (6 tablespoons) cold butter,
cut into small pieces

1 Using a sharp knife, cut incisions about 2.5 cm (1 inch) wide and 5 cm (2 inches) long, diagonally along both sides of the fish from behind the gills to the tail. Season the fish inside and out with salt and pepper then insert basil leaves into the incisions. Sprinkle the chopped fennel in the base of a heatproof dish and spoon the Tomato Concassé carefully over it.

2 Place the dish on the grill of a basket set over a wok, or in the upper part of a steamer. Cover and steam over 5 cm (2 inches) of simmering water for about 12 minutes, or until the fish is just cooked through. Remove from the heat and pour all the cooking juices that have accumulated in the dish into a frying pan (skillet). Remove the fennel trimmings, return the fish to its dish and place it back into the steamer or basket to keep hot.

3 Add the chopped shallot to the cooking juices in the frying pan and reduce the juices over a high heat until only 1 tablespoon remains. Off the heat and using a whisk, incorporate the butter, a little at a time, to thicken the sauce. Serve the fish and the sauce separately.

Freshness is the keynote, not only from a health point of view but also in the matter of flavour. Only a perfectly fresh fish has the flavour it should have. In this recipe I have combined the Chinese steaming technique with my 'fusion of flavours'. While basil and tomatoes figure equally in both Asian and European cooking, butter and fennel belong firmly in the West.
This is an excellent summer dish. It can be eaten cold also, but in that case leave out the butter sauce and serve it with a little olive oil beaten with a touch of lemon juice.

Fillets of fish
poached with ginger

Serves 4 • **preparation** 10 minutes • **cooking** 12 minutes

500 ml (2 cups) Fish Stock
(page 219)
salt and freshly ground
black pepper
1 tablespoon ginger juice
1 tablespoon fresh root ginger, cut
into fine julienne strips
450 g (1 lb) fillets of white,
firm-fleshed fish (sole, bass,
gilt-head bream, halibut, etc.)
250 ml (generous 1 cup) Tomato
Concassé (page 221)
40 g (3 tablespoons) butter
2 tablespoons finely chopped
spring onion (scallion)
2 tablespoons Shaoxing rice
wine or dry sherry

1 Bring the Fish Stock to simmering point in a saucepan. Add the salt, pepper, ginger juice and ginger julienne and leave to simmer for 2 minutes.

2 Remove from the heat, add the fish fillets and cover the pan so that the fillets poach for 5 minutes in the hot stock. Transfer them to a dish and cover with foil to keep them hot.

3 Over a high heat, reduce the cooking liquor by half then add the Tomato Concassé, butter, spring onion and rice wine and cook over a low heat for 5 minutes. Pour this sauce over the fillets and serve immediately.

In Asia, ginger is an indispensable ingredient, especially when cooking fish. Its agreeable, spicy flavour goes well with all seafood. In this recipe the fish is poached gently in a stock where it absorbs the flavours of the spices and condiments without the risk of being overcooked. Once the fish stock is prepared, the rest of the recipe is simple and produces an elegant dish with a bright red border of buttered tomato sauce. Why not serve it as the main dish for an intimate lovers' dinner, or as the entrée for a more elaborate meal?

'Crystal' prawns with
basil, peppers and garlic

Serves 2–4 • **preparation** 30 minutes • **cooking** 5 minutes

450 g (1 lb) large prawns
(shrimp), thawed and
peeled (shelled)
2 tablespoons coarse sea salt
1 tablespoon olive oil
1 tablespoon groundnut
(peanut) oil
1 large fresh red chilli (chili),
de-seeded and coarsely chopped
2 tablespoons coarsely
chopped garlic
2 tablespoons Shaoxing rice
wine or dry sherry
salt and freshly ground
black pepper
1 large handful fresh basil leaves

1 In a large bowl, mix the prawns with the salt. Leave for 30 minutes then carefully rinse them under cold running water, drain and pat dry on kitchen paper (paper towels).

2 Heat a wok, add both types of oil then the chilli, garlic and, finally, the prawns. Sauté for 1 minute, stirring constantly. Add the rice wine, season with salt and pepper and cook for a further 3 minutes, or until the prawns are cooked.

3 Finally, add the basil leaves. As soon as they have withered, mix them in to the rest of the dish. Serve immediately.

This is a quick, easy and delicious way of preparing prawns. The Chinese technique of salting them before cooking gives them a crisp texture and a more pronounced taste, while the basil, used more as a vegetable than a herb, together with the chilli and garlic, gives the whole a delicious accent of China and Provence together. Sautéing in a wok, for its part, stiffens the shellfish, keeping in all their tenderness and flavour.

A whole fish fried crisp
with tomatoes

Serves 4 • **preparation** 15 minutes • **cooking** 10 minutes

1 whole firm-fleshed fish
(sole, turbot, brill, bass, etc.)
about 1.25 kg (2 lb 12 oz),
gutted and trimmed
salt
1 teaspoon freshly ground white
pepper
1.5 litres (generous 6⅓ cups)
groundnut (peanut) oil for frying
½ packet (package) cornflour
(cornstarch)
1 head of curly endive, washed
and dried, to garnish

Fresh tomato sauce
500 ml (2 cups) Tomato Concassé
(page 221)
1 tablespoon finely chopped
fresh coriander (cilantro)
1 tablespoon olive oil
1 handful fresh basil leaves,
coarsely chopped
salt and freshly ground
black pepper

1 For the sauce, combine the Tomato Concassé, coriander, olive oil and basil in a mixing bowl. Season with salt and pepper to taste.

2 Carefully dry the fish on kitchen paper (paper towels). Along each side, at 5 cm (2 inch) intervals, make diagonal incisions about 2.5 cm (1 inch) deep and 5 cm (2 inch) long. Season the fish with salt and white pepper.

3 Heat the oil in a large wok or sauté pan until it begins to smoke. Roll the fish in the cornflour to coat it completely then shake it to remove the excess. Lower the fish into the oil with a slotted spoon and fry for 5 minutes.

4 Lift the fish out with the slotted spoon, reheat the oil until it is smoking again and lower the fish back in, frying it until it is crisp and golden.

5 Garnish a dish with the curly endive leaves, lay the fish on them and serve immediately. Serve the tomato sauce separately.

In China, a fish fried whole is often served with a sweet and sour sauce or a peppered sauce. A delicious Pacific perch, which was served to me on one occasion in Mexico, accompanied by a sauce, reminded me of this preparation. This recipe will delight those of your friends who love fried fish: the refreshing sauce offers a tasty contrast to the tender, crisp fish.

Mussels with
lemon grass butter

Serves 4–6 • **preparation** 15 minutes • **cooking** 15 minutes

1 kg (2 lb 4 oz) mussels

60 ml (¼ cup) Shaoxing rice wine or dry sherry

250 ml (generous 1 cup) Fish Stock (page 219)

2 tablespoons finely chopped shallot

3 tablespoons finely chopped lemon grass

2 tablespoons finely chopped spring onion (scallion)

1 teaspoon finely chopped fresh root ginger

1 teaspoon saffron threads

salt and freshly ground black pepper

2 tablespoons cold butter, cut into small pieces

1 Scrape and clean the mussels then wash them in several changes of very cold water. Pour the rice wine and Fish Stock into a large casserole, add the mussels, cover and cook over a high heat until all the mussels have opened. Lift them out with a slotted spoon and shell them. Discard any mussels that remain closed.

2 Filter the mussel cooking liquor through a fine sieve (strainer) into a bowl. Pour this liquor into a frying pan (skillet), together with the shallot, lemon grass, spring onion, ginger and saffron.

3 Boil for 2 minutes over a high heat then season with salt and pepper to taste. Using a whisk, incorporate the butter, a little at a time. Finally, add the shelled mussels and heat just long enough to reheat them. Serve the mussels with their sauce in soup plates.

Mussels are just as common in the kitchens of Asia as they are in Europe. Delicious and inexpensive, they can be prepared in many different ways. In China they are generally just sautéed in a wok, which is a good way of avoiding over-cooking them and giving them a rubbery texture. Personally I prefer them steamed, which only takes a few moments. The result has to be filtered to remove any grains of sand. Accompanied by a spicy sauce, Asian condiments and a touch of butter, these mussels can hold their own with the very best of mussel dishes.

Salmon fillet with ginger, basil, tomato and fine salt

Serves 4 • **preparation** 10 minutes • **cooking** 20 minutes

500 ml (2 cups) Fish Stock (page 219)

1 piece of skinned salmon fillet weighing 450 g (1 lb)

250 ml (generous 1 cup) Tomato Concassé (page 221)

2 teaspoons sesame oil

1 teaspoon finely chopped fresh root ginger

4 tablespoons finely chopped fresh basil

1 tablespoon finely chopped fresh coriander (cilantro)

fine salt for dusting

1 Bring the Fish Stock to simmering point in a saucepan. Add the salmon fillet, cover and remove from the heat. Leave to poach for 20 minutes.

2 Mix the Tomato Concassé, sesame oil, ginger, basil and coriander together in a bowl. Store in the refrigerator while the salmon is poaching.

3 Using a slotted spoon (or perhaps two slotted spoons to avoid breaking the fish) remove the salmon very carefully from the stock. (Keep the stock to use another time. Leave it to cool then store in the freezer.)

4 Cut the fillet into 4 equal portions. Place them on individual plates. Using a spoon, pour the sauce over each portion of salmon then dust it with the fine salt. Serve immediately.

They say that imitation is the sincerest form of flattery. If that is so, then this recipe is both the most flattering and the most sincere that I have ever created. The original was served to me in the Chantecler restaurant of the Hotel Negresco in Nice, at the time when James Maximin was in charge of the kitchens. It was a January day and bitterly cold; together with friends I had driven the five hour journey from Marseilles in the middle of the worst blizzard that ever fell on the south of France. You can imagine how hungry I was but, even discounting that, the magnificent salmon in coarse salt was unforgettable. Simplicity itself — a piece of salmon just poached and garnished with basil, tomatoes and coarse sea salt. I haven't sought to improve on the recipe but to adapt it using a few delicious Asian additions, such as a sauce capable of bringing out the best in the fish. This dish, at the same time as being exceptionally good (providing best quality salmon is used), is very easy to make.

A whole fish in a papillote with the flavours of Asia

Serves 2–4 • **preparation** 15 minutes • **cooking** 30 minutes

1 whole firm-fleshed fish
(bass, sole, turbot, etc.) weighing
about 1.25 kg (2 lb 12 oz),
gutted, trimmed and scaled
grey sea salt
freshly ground black pepper
8 tablespoons spring onion
(scallion), cut into julienne strips
2 tablespoons fresh root ginger,
cut into julienne strips
2 tablespoons finely chopped
fresh coriander (cilantro)
1 fresh red chilli (chili), de-seeded
and cut into julienne strips
60 g (4½ tablespoons) cold butter
2 tablespoons light soy sauce

1 Preheat the oven to 200°C (400°F, Gas Mark 6). Cut a rectangle of foil 30 cm (12 inches) wide and 15 cm (6 inches) longer than the fish. Rub the fish with salt and freshly ground black pepper on both sides then lay it on the foil.

2 Sprinkle the spring onion, ginger, coriander and chilli over it, distribute the butter over the fish in little pieces and pour over the soy sauce. Carefully close up the papillote, sealing the ends.

3 Place the papillote on a baking sheet and bake for about 30 minutes, or until the fish can easily be pierced to the centre with a bamboo skewer. Bring the fish to the table on a dish, still in its papillote, and open it at table. Serve each portion accompanied by the herbs from the papillote.

Steaming is a well-tried method of preparing a whole fish, in the East as well as the West. In Asia it is usually seasoned with the winning trio: garlic, ginger and chives. In France at one time, and even today, a paper envelope spread with oil or butter was the only known way to steam a fish. Today, the paper has been replaced by foil. While not as romantic as the paper version, it seals more effectively, insulates better and retains the moisture. In addition, foil is always readily available. Cooked this way, the fish stays moist and full-flavoured, tender and delicately impregnated with the Asian herbs that accompany it. The emergence of a whole fish from its papillote makes a big effect at table if you have guests, but you can adapt this recipe for use with fish fillets or steaks by reducing the length of time in the oven by half.

Spicy prawns stewed with ginger

Serves 4 • **preparation** 30 minutes • **cooking** 10 minutes

700 g (1 lb 9 oz) raw prawns (shrimp)
2 teaspoons coarse salt
1 tablespoon butter
1 tablespoon extra virgin olive oil
2 tablespoons finely chopped shallot
2 tablespoons finely chopped spring onion (scallion)
2 teaspoons fresh red chilli (chili), finely chopped
2 tablespoons finely chopped fresh root ginger
1 medium turnip, peeled, cut into dice
1 medium carrot, peeled, cut into small dice
120 ml (½ cup) dry white wine
60 ml (¼ cup) Shaoxing rice wine or dry sherry
250 ml (generous 1 cup) Fish Stock (page 219)
2 tablespoons single (light) cream
120 ml (½ cup) Tomato Concassé (page 221)
freshly ground black pepper
3 tablespoons finely chopped fresh coriander (cilantro)

1 Place the prawns (thawed, peeled (shelled) and the black vein removed) and the coarse salt into a bowl. Mix together and leave for 30 minutes then rinse the prawns thoroughly under cold running water and pat them dry on kitchen paper (paper towels).

2 Heat the butter and olive oil in a wok or a cast-iron sauté pan. Add the shallot, spring onion, chilli and ginger and sauté for 2 minutes. Add the turnip and carrot dice and sauté for a further 2 minutes. Add the wine and rice wine, and reduce almost completely, then add the Fish Stock and reduce by one third.

3 Finally add the prawns, cream and Tomato Concassé. Season with salt and pepper to taste. Cook for 5 minutes, stirring constantly. Add the coriander, stir well and serve immediately.

The French word ragoût, *meaning stew, has its roots in words meaning something that re-awakens the appetite and invites one to indulge oneself. One can, therefore, define a* ragoût *as a mixture of ingredients (meat, fish and/or vegetables) cooked in an appetizing way. Every region of France prides itself on its traditional stews, which are not dissimilar to those of China, where stews are cooked in the damp, steamy interior of an earthenware pot.*

Abalone sautéed with broccoli

Serves 2 • **preparation** 10 minutes • **cooking** 10 minutes

450 g (1 lb) broccoli
salt
200 g (7 oz) of the white part
of fresh abalone or scallops,
cleaned by the fishmonger
1 tablespoon groundnut
(peanut) oil
1 tablespoon coarsely
chopped garlic
120 ml (½ cup) crème fraîche
(or sour cream)
1 tablespoon oyster sauce

1 Separate the broccoli heads into little florets. Peel the stems and cut into rounds (circles). Boil them in salted water for 3 minutes and immediately plunge them into iced water. Drain them carefully.

2 Trim the abalone or scallops and cut them into fine strips. If using abalone, pound these several times with a mallet or the flat of a cleaver to tenderize them (scallops do not need this treatment).

3 Heat a wok or sauté pan and add the oil then the garlic, broccoli and, finally, the strips of abalone. Sauté them for 30 seconds, mixing constantly. Remove the strips of abalone with a slotted spoon and set them aside. Pour the crème fraîche and the oyster sauce into the wok and cook for 2 minutes. Return the abalone to the sauce and mix again. Serve immediately.

Abalone, fresh, dried or canned, has a distinguished place in Asian cuisine. In Europe, where it is less common than in Asia, it is costly and highly prized. The texture and delicate flavour of this shellfish is truly delicious when it is not over-cooked, and cooking in a wok is one of the methods which gives the best results. If fresh abalone is hard to find and outrageously expensive, replace it with scallops. Broccoli is a traditional accompaniment for abalone and it goes equally well with scallops, which are complemented by its flavour. As to the unusual combination of crème fraîche and oyster sauce, it really does honour to the flavour of these delicious shellfish.

Salmon wrapped in Chinese cabbage leaves and steamed

Serves 4 • **preparation** 12 minutes • **cooking** 6–8 minutes

1 Chinese (Napa) cabbage

4 salmon steaks, skinned, about 120 g (4¼ oz) each

salt and freshly ground black pepper

2 tablespoons finely chopped fresh coriander (cilantro)

4 tablespoons Fish Stock (page 219)

2 teaspoons lemon or lime juice

75 g (6 tablespoons) cold butter, cut into small pieces

fresh coriander sprigs, to garnish

1 Remove some of the large cabbage leaves, keeping them as whole as possible. Blanch them in boiling water for just long enough to make them supple. Drain them and dry on kitchen paper (paper towels) and spread them on the work surface.

2 Lay a salmon steak on the end of one of the leaves (use 2 leaves if one is too small), sprinkle it generously with salt, pepper and fresh coriander. Roll the leaf around the salmon, tucking in the edges as you go.

3 Lay the cabbage parcels in a deep, heatproof dish and place in the basket of a wok or the upper part of a steamer. Steam gently for 6–8 minutes.

4 Remove the dish from the wok or steamer and drain the cooking juices into a small saucepan. Add the Fish Stock and lemon juice and reduce this by one third over a high heat then add the butter, a little at a time, while whisking constantly. Adjust the seasoning with more salt and pepper if needed. Serve the salmon parcels coated in the sauce, garnished with coriander sprigs.

Fresh salmon is undeniably an attractive medium for cooks: its firm texture, beautiful colour and exquisite flavour – delicate but characteristic – are all very seductive. Its flavour is a combination of strength and subtlety. It is noble enough to stand up to a spicy sauce, as in the recipe for Salmon Fillet with Ginger, Basil, Tomato and Fine Salt (page 68), *while at the same time lending itself to simpler ways of preparing it, such as the above, in which it is steamed gently in a wrapping of Chinese cabbage leaves. The cabbage helps to preserve the tenderness of the flesh, at the same time imbuing it with a slight sweetness of its own.*

Fish steamed with spring onions and garlic shoots

Serves 4 • **preparation** 5 minutes • **cooking** 5 minutes

4 halibut fillet steaks,
500 g (1 lb 2 oz) in total
salt and freshly ground
black pepper
4 tablespoons spring onion
(scallion), cut into julienne strips
4 tablespoons garlic shoots,
cut into julienne strips
120 ml (½ cup) Fish Stock
(page 219)
30 g (2 tablespoons) cold butter,
cut into small pieces

1 Season the halibut steaks with salt and pepper. Lay them on a heatproof dish and sprinkle them liberally with the julienne of spring onion and garlic shoots. Place the dish in a wok basket or the upper part of a steamer and steam gently for 5 minutes.

2 Pour the accumulated cooking juices into a small saucepan and return the fish to the covered basket to keep hot. Add the Fish Stock to the juices in the saucepan and reduce them by half. Add the butter a little at a time, whisking constantly, then dress the fish on a serving dish, cover with the herbs and serve coated with the sauce.

I discovered young garlic shoots in the South of France. They immediately appealed to me. While not so firm as their elder relatives — garlic cloves — their flavour shows through with great clarity. Garlic shoots seem to have a special affinity for ingredients with a subtle flavour. The Chinese adore garlic shoots — as I was to discover later in Hong Kong — and make particular use of them when cooking with a wok. At all events, steaming manages to bring out the best of the flavours, both of the fish and the garlic shoots, without either dominating.
This delicious dish is utterly simple to prepare if garlic shoots are available. If you can't find them, use chives instead.

Prawns sautéed with
mustard and coriander

Serves 4 • **preparation** 4 minutes • **cooking** 5 minutes

30 g (2 tablespoons) butter
2 teaspoons groundnut
(peanut) oil
700 g (1 lb 9 oz) large prawns
(shrimp), fresh or thawed
2 tablespoons coarsely
chopped garlic
salt and freshly ground
black pepper
2 tablespoons Shaoxing rice
wine or dry sherry
120 ml (½ cup) Fish Stock
(page 219)
2 tablespoons finely chopped
fresh coriander (cilantro)
2 tablespoons Dijon mustard

1 Heat the butter and oil in a wok or sauté pan. Add the prawns (peeled (shelled) and de-veined) and the garlic. Sauté for 1 minute, stirring with a spatula. Season with salt and pepper to taste.

2 Add the rice wine, Fish Stock, coriander and mustard. Cook for 2 minutes over a high heat, or just until the prawns are cooked. Serve immediately.

The better the quality of the ingredients, the more of a feast the result will be. Here we have big, fat, pink, firm-fleshed prawns, dressed in a touch of mustard and fresh coriander, a touch of rice wine, olive oil and fish stock. All go to make a very simple, delectable and original dish. Fresh gambas (tiger prawns) are recommended for this dish, but you could also use frozen prawns.

Crab pancakes with
Asian spices

Makes about 16 pancakes • **preparation** 20 minutes • **cooking** 15 minutes

110 g (generous ¾ cup) flour

2 eggs

1 tablespoon sesame oil

2 teaspoons salt

freshly ground black pepper

2 teaspoons finely chopped
fresh root ginger

3 tablespoons finely chopped
spring onions (scallions),
plus extra to garnish

250 ml (generous 1 cup) milk

2 tablespoons lemon juice

200 g (7 oz) fresh crabmeat
(shelled crab or spider crab)

groundnut (peanut) oil to
fry the pancakes (crêpes)

1 Mix the flour, eggs, sesame oil, salt, pepper, ginger, spring onion, milk and lemon juice in a large bowl. Finally add the crabmeat.

2 Heat a little groundnut oil in a non-stick frying pan (skillet) and pour in about 60–70 ml (4 tablespoons) of the batter. Over a medium heat, brown slightly on the first side, then turn the pancake and brown it on the other. Serve immediately, garnished with chopped spring onions, or leave in a warm oven until ready to serve.

Pancakes are universal, but they vary from country to country. In China they are reduced to their most basic form — flour and water. I find the French version softer-textured and lighter and also better flavoured and more adaptable to different ways of serving them. Here, for example, I have combined crabmeat with Asian herbs to create a delicious dish, which has the extra advantage of making a small amount of crab — an expensive ingredient, as you know — go quite a long way. Serve these crab pancakes with other fish dishes, such as Mussels with Lemon Grass Butter (page 66), or on their own, with a little butter and lemon juice.

Fish soup flavoured
with ginger

Serves 4–6 • **preparation** 30 minutes • **cooking** 20 minutes

1 kg (2 lb 4 oz) firm fish fillets

2 litres (8½ cups) Fish Stock (page 219)

2 thick slices fresh root ginger

750 ml (3 cups) Tomato Concassé (page 221)

250 g (9 oz) sugar snap peas, topped and tailed (trimmed) and de-stringed

60 g (2¼ oz) fresh kumquats, coarsely chopped

Garlic mayonnaise with chilli (chili) and Sichuan pepper (glossary, page 239)

fresh coriander (cilantro) sprigs, to garnish

Marinade

2 teaspoons fine salt

2 tablespoons finely chopped coriander

2 tablespoons finely chopped spring onion (scallion)

1 tablespoon ginger juice

1 teaspoon sesame oil

freshly ground black pepper

1 Cut the fish fillets (bass, sole, monkfish (angler fish), halibut, etc.) into pieces 2.5 × 5 cm (1 × 2 inches). Combine all the marinade ingredients in a bowl and add the fish, mix well and leave in a cool place to marinate for 30 minutes.

2 Bring the Fish Stock to the boil in a casserole. Add the ginger and leave it to simmer for 15 minutes then remove it with a slotted spoon.

3 Place the marinated fish into the stock and simmer for 2 minutes then add the Tomato Concassé, sugar peas and kumquats. Cook over a low heat for a further 3–4 minutes. Garnish with coriander sprigs and serve with the spiced mayonnaise.

Fish soups and stews are for the most part a speciality of the West, although fish soups are appreciated in both hemispheres. With this dish, I am not offering a Bouillabaisse — my benchmark for this type of cooking — but an East–West variation on a theme; a full-flavoured, attractive dish, worthy of being enjoyed for its own sake. The ginger dominates, its fresh and piquant note offering a counterpoint to the fish.

Sautéed prawns with
carrots and asparagus

Serves 2–4 • **preparation** 15 minutes • **cooking** 5 minutes

Bok choy

1 tablespoon balsamic vinegar

1½ tablespoons extra virgin olive oil

salt and freshly ground
black pepper

225 g (8 oz) *bok choy* (a type of
Chinese cabbage)

Prawns (Shrimp)

120 ml (½ cup) Chicken Stock
(page 218)

1 tablespoon groundnut (peanut) oil

2 teaspoons olive oil

450 g (1 lb) raw pink prawns

225 g (8 oz) small new carrots, peeled
and blanched

225 g (8 oz) asparagus, peeled, cut
into 6 cm (2½ inch) lengths and
blanched

2 teaspoons finely chopped fresh
root ginger

1 tablespoon shallot

2 tablespoons Shaoxing rice
wine or dry sherry

salt and freshly ground black pepper

1 Pour the Chicken Stock into a small pan over a high heat and reduce to 2 tablespoons. Set aside.

2 To make the *bok choy*, place the vinegar, olive oil, salt and pepper into a bowl. Add the *bok choy* washed, cut into small pieces and briefly blanched in boiling water, mix and spread in a dish.

3 For the prawns: heat the groundnut and olive oils in a wok or large frying pan (skillet) and sauté the prawns (peeled (shelled) and de-veined) for 1 minute, stirring constantly, then remove them with a slotted spoon and set aside. In the wok, sauté the carrots and asparagus with the finely chopped ginger and the shallot, finely chopped, the rice wine and salt and pepper, stirring constantly, for 2 minutes. Add the reduced Chicken Stock then the prawns. Sauté for a further 2 minutes. Using a spoon, arrange the prawns on the *bok choy* and serve immediately.

In this simple but appetizing dish, rich in contrasting colours, textures and flavours, the Asian and European ingredients mix in the most natural way imaginable, each keeping its own character. Once again, it is a quick and easy to make dish. You can serve it hot, or at room temperature in the heat of the summer.

Scallops with three kinds of mushrooms

Serves 4 • **preparation** 15 minutes • **cooking** 6–7 minutes

50 g (1¾ oz) black Chinese mushrooms, soaked for 20 minutes then drained
2 tablespoons olive oil
100 g (3½ oz) sugar snap peas, topped and tailed (trimmed) and washed
1 red (bell) pepper about 100 g (3½ oz) in weight, cut into strips
450 g (1 lb) fresh scallops with their coral, trimmed
4 fresh kumquats finely sliced
1 teaspoon ginger juice
salt and freshly ground black pepper
250 ml (generous 1 cup) Fish Stock (page 219)
30 g (2 tablespoons) butter
100 g (3½ oz) oyster mushrooms or button (white) mushrooms, peeled
100 g (3½ oz) enokitake (small white Japanese mushrooms, see glossary page 4), to garnish

1 Remove the tough end of the stalks of the black mushrooms. Cut them into julienne strips. Heat the olive oil in a wok or sauté pan and sauté the sugar peas and the strips of pepper for 1 minute. Add the scallops, kumquats, ginger juice and salt and pepper. Cook until the scallops turn opaque and are almost firm then remove them from the wok and keep hot.

2 In a small saucepan, reduce the Fish Stock by one third. Clean the wok and return it to the heat. When it is up to temperature add the butter and all the mushrooms (except the enokitake) and sauté for 2 minutes. Add the Fish Stock and cook for a further 3 minutes, or until the mushrooms are tender.

3 Arrange the scallops and vegetables in the centre of a dish and surround them with the mushrooms. Garnish the edge of the dish with the enokitake and serve immediately.

I have tried, here, to unite Asian and Western ingredients in such a way that each one respects and remains on good terms with its neighbours. The flavours each have their own personality but don't encroach one on the other. The result is a delicious shellfish dish, which is a treat for the eye as well as the taste buds.

Jade prawns with flat-leaf parsley, coriander and basil

Serves 4 • **preparation** 5 minutes • **cooking** 7–8 minutes

2 tablespoons extra virgin olive oil

750 g (1 lb 10 oz) raw prawns (shrimp)

2 tablespoons finely chopped fresh coriander (cilantro)

1 tablespoon finely chopped fresh flat-leaf parsley

3 tablespoons finely chopped fresh basil

2 tablespoons coarsely chopped garlic

3 tablespoons finely chopped spring onion (scallion)

salt and freshly ground black pepper

fresh basil sprigs, to garnish

1 Heat the olive oil in a wok or large sauté pan. Add the prawns (thawed but shell on) and sauté them for 5 minutes over a high heat, stirring with a spatula.

2 Add the rest of the ingredients and sauté for a further 2 minutes, coating the prawns liberally with the chopped herbs. Serve immediately, garnished with basil.

The word 'jade' refers to the colour of the herbs that make up the dish, as in a similar dish I discovered in Hong Kong. The bright pink tones of the prawns stand out against the dark green of the coriander, parsley and basil. As you will find for yourself if you try this dish, the Asian and Western flavours mingle together most harmoniously. This dish is a delight to the eye as well as the palate. Prawns are particularly succulent cooked in their shells.

Shellfish, butter sauce
and black beans

Serves 4 • **preparation** 15 minutes • **cooking** 35 minutes

450 g (1 lb) live mussels

450 g (1 lb) fresh cockles or clams

250 ml (generous 1 cup) Chicken Stock (page 218)

1 tablespoon fermented black beans, chopped

500 ml (2 cups) Tomato concassé (page 221)

30 g (2 tablespoons) cold butter, cut into small pieces

1 handful fresh basil leaves, to garnish

1 Scrape the mussels and the cockles or clams and wash them very carefully in several changes of water. The cockles or clams may need to be left in salt water for 1 hour to rid them of any sand

2 Heat the Chicken Stock and black beans in a large casserole. Add the mussels and clams, cover and cook over a high heat for 2–3 minutes until they have opened. Remove them with a slotted spoon and set aside. Discard any that are still closed.

3 Filter the cooking liquor and reduce it by half over a high heat. Add the Tomato Concassé and cook for 30 minutes. Incorporate the butter, a little at a time, whisking constantly, then add the shellfish to the sauce and reheat for 1 minute.

4 Pour the contents of the casserole into a deep dish and garnish with the basil leaves. Serve immediately.

To people like me who adore shellfish, cockles and mussels have all the salty, piquant flavour of the sea, and the black beans bring this particularly well to the fore. This condiment is actually used in China to bring out flavours, especially of seafood. In a slightly heretical manner (from a Chinese point of view) I have included tomatoes, basil and butter, to give this dish its rich and complex aroma.

Poultry

Peking duck

Grilled chicken with *hoisin* sauce

Braised chicken legs with tomato-ginger sauce

Grilled chicken legs with mustard

Boned and roasted turkey

Rice stuffing with herbs

Roast chicken with ginger and orange

Chicken with mushroom stuffing

Chicken wings roasted with peppers

Young cockerel fried with spices

Chicken in two courses:
  - Breast of chicken cooked with Shaoxing rice wine, butter and Sichuan pepper
  - Chicken legs marinated and grilled, Asian-style parsley vinaigrette

Pigeons 'lacquered' with honey

Boned and stuffed quail

Stewed pigeon with Chinese vegetables

Pigeon stuffed with cornbread

Cornbread with ginger and chilli

Duck served as two courses

Braised duck

Peking duck 'lacquered' with orange

Fricassee of chicken

Quail, marinated and grilled

Creamed breast of chicken with red peppers and *bok choy*

Spatchcocked marinated pigeon with Shaoxing rice wine sauce

Chicken sautéed with sugar snap peas and water chestnuts

Marinated chicken coated with sesame seeds

Chicken

This is the king of poultry, universal and inexpensive, enjoyed by all. It is so common that we tend to underestimate it and imagine that there is no more to discover about all its great qualities. Chicken is cheap, easily digested and low in cholesterol and calories, but familiarity breeds indifference. It is worth bringing to mind how delicious a well-prepared chicken can be. When we have finished praising the nobility of the duck, the generosity of the turkey and the delicacy of feathered game, we always come back to the humble chicken, which never disappoints. I do stress the words 'well-prepared', though; given modern farming methods, chicken today is less full-flavoured and not as firm-fleshed as it used to be in the past but, happily, it is once again becoming possible to find good-quality chicken. I recommend that you always buy the best farm-raised ones.

In China, peasant nation par excellence, people have lived for millennia in harmony with nature and creation. Chicken there has an almost religious significance. During my childhood, this idea was firmly instilled in me. I not only ate chicken, I read about it, studied it, learnt, meditated and inwardly digested it in all its symbolic dimensions. All this left me with an unfailing respect for this familiar but providential fowl. For example, chicken must be very carefully cooked if it is to stay tender and succulent. This is particularly so in the case of roast chicken. In Asia, chicken is rarely cooked in this way; it is more likely to be braised, poached, fried or steamed. When it is roasted, this is usually done in a salt crust, a technique which retains all its tenderness without salting it excessively. Roasting is used much more frequently in the West. It does, however, pose the usual problem that arises when cooking with dry heat – the meat risks becoming dry too. Which is why cooking on a spit is preferable to oven roasting because it allows the bird to be basted constantly to retain its moisture.

My friend, chef Jacques Pépin, taught me an incomparable technique: roast the chicken upside-down (breast underneath). The juices sink down into the breast meat and keep it tender. Towards the end of cooking, turn it over and finish browning it evenly. This somewhat unorthodox method gives excellent results. As to chicken legs, they lend themselves admirably to grilling (broiling) since their meat needs a fairly long cooking time and responds well to highly spiced marinades.

A word on the young cockerel: this little bird is generally inexpensive and easy to prepare. It improves for being marinated prior to cooking. Deep-fried (see Young Cockerel Fried with Spices, page 100), it can be delicious.

Turkey

The volatile American turkey made its appearance in France after the French Revolution when Brillat-Savarin, back from exile in New England, introduced it to his compatriots. Though it requires just as much care and delicacy as chicken, it is frequently ill-used. Too often it is dried out by overcooking. I recommend a mixture of techniques to avoid this. The turkey should first be boned and steamed (to retain the tenderness and flavour), then finished off in the oven to give the skin an appetizing golden sheen. I don't need to tell you that you should always buy a free-range bird fed on a cereal-based diet, preferably an organically raised one.

Duck, quail and pigeon, etc.

Duck needs no introduction. From Peking duck to the French Canard à l'Orange, this marvellous bird has inspired some of the world's best dishes. The duck recipes I present in this book are examples of the best flavours and culinary techniques of both East and West.

In Japan, the quail is regarded as the king of game. It would be eaten to a much greater extent in China, too, were it not that pheasants abound in that country. In Europe, too, quail is greatly appreciated but here, as elsewhere, it is difficult to buy the lean, firm wild ones; one finds only farmed birds, which are fatter but still full of flavour. When it comes to cooking other game birds – woodcock, thrush, partridge – there is nothing better than the traditional method to bring out their flavour: coat the bird with butter or wrap in a sheet of bacon fat and roast it in a high heat over a slice of bread, basting it frequently (the bread serves to soak up the cooking juices).

Pigeon is becoming increasingly popular, and rightly so. This bird has a flavour and texture all of its own, far removed from the relatively neutral qualities of the chicken. In China, notably in the Canton region, the pigeon is an object of veneration. When I was a child I had the opportunity to eat it quite often, but only at family banquets, since it is expensive. It was always an unforgettable experience. The pigeons were briefly cooked in a braising sauce then air-dried and fried at the last moment. The contrast between the crisp skin and the tender meat was a delight.

Peking duck

Serves 4–6 • **preparation** 2–5 hours • **cooking** 1 hour

3 tablespoons *hoisin* sauce
1 tablespoon dried thyme
2 teaspoons salt flavoured with
Sichuan pepper
(glossary, page 237)
1 duck, weighing about 1.5 kg
(3 lb 5 oz), prepared in the same
way as Spatchcocked,
Marinated Pigeon (page 120)
250 ml (generous 1 cup) water

Lacquer
2 litres (8½ cups) water
3 tablespoons honey
3 tablespoons spicy soy sauce

1 Mix the *hoisin* sauce, thyme and salt flavoured with Sichuan pepper together. Rub it around the inside of the duck.

2 Place the ingredients for the lacquer in a saucepan and bring to the boil. Remove from the heat and pour over the skin of the duck. Repeat this process several times then leave the duck to dry in a cool, airy place for about 5 hours, or 2 hours in front of a fan. Correctly dried, the duck skin should have the appearance of parchment.

3 Preheat the oven to 200°C (400°F, Gas Mark 6). Place the duck, skin-side up, on a grid in a roasting tin (pan), with the 250 ml (generous 1 cup) water. Roast for 1 hour, or until the skin is crisp and a deep reddish-brown colour. Carve the duck and serve immediately.

The French word laquée *(lacquered) is very descriptive of the result: the skin of the duck is shiny, crisp and full of flavour. This is due to the marinade based on soy sauce and honey. Inside the duck more magic is produced by the* hoisin *sauce, thyme and Sichuan pepper salt mixture. It is one of my favourite duck recipes. The instructions are given for roasting in the oven, but nothing prevents you from cooking on the embers on a barbecue, as long as you are careful not to let it burn.*

Grilled chicken with
hoisin sauce

Serves 2–4 • **preparation** 30 minutes • **cooking** 5 minutes

4 chicken breasts about
100 g (3½ oz) each

Marinade

2 teaspoons fresh thyme, rubbed
3 tablespoons *hoisin* sauce
2 tablespoons Shaoxing rice
wine or dry sherry
1 tablespoon extra virgin olive oil
salt and freshly ground
black pepper

1 Mix all the ingredients for the marinade together in a deep dish and rub it into the chicken breasts on both sides. Wrap the chicken breasts in clingfilm (plastic wrap) and marinate for 30 minutes at room temperature or 1 hour in the refrigerator. In the latter case, leave them to come back to room temperature before grilling.

2 Light the barbecue or heat the grill (broiler). When the grill is hot or the embers have turned whitish, briefly cook the chicken breasts on both sides, without overcooking them.

Nothing is better than hoisin *sauce for bringing out the rather neutral flavour of a modern chicken. It just needs diluting (done here with a little rice wine and olive oil) to be sure that it enhances rather than nullifies the flavour. You could ring the changes by replacing the* hoisin sauce *by Chinese plum sauce (see page 12 of glossary). These chicken breasts are delicious cold, on a picnic or as part of a buffet. Cut into thin slices they would make a flavoursome and original chicken salad. Finally, they go well with* Cubed Tomatoes with Tarragon and Sesame Oil *(page 38).*

Braised chicken legs with
tomato-ginger sauce

Serves 2–4 • **preparation** 15 minutes • **cooking** 30 minutes

1 tablespoon olive oil

750 g (1 lb 10 oz) whole chicken legs (about 6), separated into thighs and drumsticks

salt and freshly ground black pepper

1 large can peeled tomatoes, coarsely chopped

2 tablespoons coarsely chopped garlic

1 tablespoon finely chopped fresh root ginger

1 small fresh red chilli (chili), de-seeded and chopped

2 teaspoons sugar

3 tablespoons finely chopped fresh coriander (cilantro)

1 Heat the olive oil in a wok or medium-sized frying pan over a medium heat. Brown the chicken on both sides, skin side first. When you turn them over, season with salt and pepper while the other side is browning. Drain them on kitchen paper (paper towels) and set aside.

2 Pour away all but 2 teaspoons of the oil from the pan. Add the tomatoes, garlic, ginger, chilli, sugar, salt and pepper. Cook over a fairly high heat for 8 minutes then reduce the heat and leave to simmer. Add the chicken, cover and braise over a low heat for 20 minutes. Add the coriander just before serving.

A tomato sauce well flavoured with ginger goes marvellously with chicken legs. Each of the flavours asserts itself, but the three together make a delicious dish that can be reheated if any is left over. Some say it is even better the following day.

Grilled chicken legs
with mustard

Serves 4 • **preparation** 12 minutes • **cooking** 30–40 minutes

700 g (1 lb 9 oz) whole chicken
legs (about 6), divided into
thighs and drumsticks
1 teaspoon coarse salt
freshly ground black pepper
fresh herbs, to garnish

Marinade
1 tablespoon finely chopped garlic
1 teaspoon finely chopped fresh
root ginger
4 spring onions (scallions),
finely chopped
2 tablespoons Dijon mustard
2 tablespoons sesame oil
50 g (1¾ oz) fresh kumquats,
cut into thin slices,
plus extra to garnish

1 Season the chicken all over with the salt and pepper. Mix all the marinade ingredients together and blend them to a smooth paste. Using a spatula, coat the chicken pieces all over with the marinade, wrap them in clingfilm (plastic wrap) and leave in the refrigerator for at least 2 hours.

2 Thirty minutes before grilling (broiling) the chicken, take it out of the refrigerator. Grill the pieces skin-side down under a grill (broiler), turning them over when the skin has become crisp. Alternatively, light the barbecue and cook over hot embers.
As soon as the meat is firm and can be easily pierced with a wooden skewer, it is cooked. Remove from the grill and leave to rest for 5 minutes before serving, garnished with slices of kumquat and fresh herbs.

I love chicken legs for their strong flavour and firm texture. They lend themselves to all the whims and spicy marinades of East and West. Here I have combined the two top Asian ingredients – ginger and spring onions – and teamed them with garlic and mustard. The kumquats lift the flavour of the sauce and the chicken with their fine, citrus taste. You could add fresh herbs to the marinade, such as thyme or tarragon. Olive oil could replace the sesame oil. One word of warning – be careful with the ginger. If you add too much it will dominate the other ingredients and unbalance the whole dish. These grilled chicken legs are delicious cold, which makes them perfect for a picnic.

Boned and roasted
turkey

Serves 8–12 • **preparation** 50 minutes • **cooking** 2 hours

1 farm-reared turkey
weighing about 5 kg (11 lb)
(make Turkey and Poultry Stock
(page 220) with the bones)
3 tablespoons coarse sea salt
1 tablespoon freshly ground
black pepper
3 tablespoons sesame oil
120 ml (½ cup) lemon juice

Stuffing
Rice Stuffing with Herbs that you
can prepare and leave to cool
completely after boning the
turkey (page 95)

Sauce
1 litre (4 cups) Turkey and Poultry
Stock (page 220)
salt and freshly ground
black pepper

1 To bone the turkey, make an incision along the full length of the neck to uncover the wishbone then cut through the wing joints with scissors without cutting the flesh. Release the bones and the carcass, scraping and pushing the flesh away as you go. Cut the leg joints in the same way as the wings and loosen the meat from the leg bones. Finally detach the rump and the rest of the carcass. Scrape the bones of the thighs and drumsticks to detach them completely.

2 Sew up the turkey from the rump to the neck, leaving a 6–8 cm (2½–3¼ inch) opening through which to insert the stuffing. Coat it outside and in with salt and pepper, sesame oil and 2 tablespoons of lemon juice. Place the turkey in a large glass bowl, pour over the rest of the lemon juice, cover with clingfilm (plastic wrap) and leave overnight in the refrigerator.

3 Remove the turkey from the marinade and pat it with kitchen paper (paper towels).

4 Fill with the stuffing and sew up the opening. Tie the turkey with string as for a roast.

5 Place a grid in the base of a large, cast-iron casserole, cover with a heatproof dish and place the turkey on it, breast-side up. Pour water into the casserole to a depth of 4 cm (1½ inches) and bring to the boil. Reduce the heat and steam the turkey gently for 1½ hours. Pierce the breast with a thin wooden skewer: when the juices run clear it is cooked. Towards the end of the cooking time, preheat the oven to 240°C (475°F, Gas Mark 9). Remove the turkey from the casserole and reserve the cooking juices. Empty the water from the casserole, replace the grid and lay the turkey on it. Roast it in the oven for 15–20 minutes. While it is roasting, pour the stock, together with the turkey cooking juices, into a saucepan and reduce for about 8 minutes until 750 ml (3 cups) remain. Skim it well as it boils. Pass through a sieve (strainer) and season with salt and pepper. Serve the turkey and sauce together.

You may find this recipe complicated, but a turkey is a worthy bird and should be prepared with care.

Rice stuffing
with herbs

Makes about 2 kg (4 lb 8 oz) stuffing • **preparation** 15 minutes • **cooking** 15 minutes

2 tablespoons groundnut (peanut) oil
150 g (5 oz) shallots, finely chopped
75 g (2¾ oz) spring onions (scallions), finely chopped
130 ml (generous ½ cup) Shaoxing rice wine or dry sherry
450 g (1 lb) Chinese sausages, diced
675 g (3⅜ cups) glutinous rice
750 ml (3 cups) Turkey and Poultry Stock (page 220)
1 teaspoon salt
freshly ground black pepper
750 g (1 lb 10 oz) water chestnuts (fresh or canned), peeled and diced
1 small red (bell) pepper, de-seeded and diced
1½ teaspoons fresh tarragon leaves
1 teaspoon fresh thyme
3 tablespoons finely chopped chives
3 tablespoons finely chopped fresh coriander (cilantro)

1 Place the glutinous rice in a bowl, cover with water and leave to soak overnight then drain carefully.

2 In a large wok or sauté pan, heat the groundnut oil over a fairly high heat. Fry the shallots and spring onions for about 30 seconds then add the rice wine. Reduce it almost completely. Add the sausages, stir and sauté for 1 minute. Add the rice, Turkey and Poultry Stock and the salt and pepper. Cover and cook for about 8 minutes, or until all the liquid is absorbed, shaking the pan from time to time to stop the rice from sticking.

3 Add the water chestnuts, pepper, tarragon, thyme, chives and coriander and cook for 3 minutes, stirring frequently. Remove from the heat and leave to cool to room temperature.

4 To stuff the turkey you will need about 1 kg (2 lb 4 oz) of stuffing, and a large chicken would need 500 g (1 lb 2 oz). You could put the rest in a greased gratin dish and bake it for 45 minutes in the oven preheated to 180°C (350°F, Gas Mark 4).

While it is resolutely Asian, this stuffing is perfectly at home on Western menus, in particular those for Christmas and New Year; the traditional period for turkey. There, too, the preparation can almost all be done in advance. This stuffing also goes very well with chicken.

Roast chicken with
ginger and orange

Serves 2–4 • **preparation** 15 minutes • **cooking** 1 hour 20 minutes

1 farm-reared or organic
chicken weighing about
2.25–2.5 kg (5–5 lb 8 oz)
salt and freshly ground
black pepper
400 ml (1¾ cups) Chicken Stock
(page 218, optional)

Flavourings
1 whole orange,
cut into 10 segments
10 garlic cloves, crushed
but not peeled
12 fresh thyme sprigs
5 thin slices fresh root
ginger, unpeeled
1 handful fresh coriander (cilantro)

1 Preheat the oven to 230°C (450°F, Gas Mark 8). Season the chicken inside and out with salt and pepper. Place the orange segments, garlic, thyme, ginger and coriander in a bowl and mix carefully. Close the neck cavity of the chicken with a bamboo skewer. Pack the mixture firmly into the chicken and skewer the other aperture closed too.

2 Place the chicken, breast down, on a grid in a roasting tin (pan) and roast for 15 minutes. Reduce the oven temperature to 180°C (350°F, Gas Mark 4) and roast for a further 40 minutes. Increase the oven temperature to 230°C (450°F, Gas Mark 8), turn the chicken over and cook for 5 minutes to brown the skin of the breasts.

3 If you want to make a quick sauce, remove the aromatic ingredients from the inside of the chicken and leave them to simmer for 20 minutes in the Chicken Stock. Pass through a fine sieve (strainer) then return to the pan and reduce by half over a high heat. Remove the chicken from the oven and leave to rest for 15 minutes before carving.

Roast chicken is undoubtedly one of the easiest and cheapest main dishes to make. It can also be one of the best if it is well prepared and doesn't risk drying out. I would remind you of the method I mentioned in the introduction to this chapter: first roast the chicken, breast-side down, then turn it over towards the end of cooking to brown it. I also put the herbs and spices inside the bird, either by themselves or as part of a stuffing. In the first case they can be removed just before the chicken has finished cooking and boiled for a few minutes in reduced stock to make an excellent sauce. Pass it through a sieve before serving. This chicken is perfect cold, for a picnic or a light meal.

Chicken with
mushroom stuffing

Serves 6–8 • **preparation** 15 minutes • **cooking** 1 hour

2 farm-raised or organic chickens weighing about 2.25 kg (5 lb) each

Stuffing
450 g (1 lb) button (white) mushrooms, washed and wiped
450 g (1 lb) fresh shiitake or 100 g (3½ oz) dried black mushrooms
30 g (2 tablespoons) butter
2 tablespoons olive oil
salt and freshly ground black pepper
50 g (1 cup) breadcrumbs
3 handfuls fresh basil leaves or parsley, washed and dried
2 tablespoons fresh marjoram leaves

1 If using black mushrooms, soak them in a bowl of hot water until they are pliable. Wipe the button mushrooms. If you use shiitake, cut off the tough ends of the stalks.

2 Coarsely chop the button mushrooms and the shiitake. Heat the butter and oil in a large frying pan or wok, season the mushrooms with salt and pepper and leave them to sweat over a medium heat for 5 minutes until the water that runs from them has almost evaporated. Add the breadcrumbs, basil, marjoram and check the seasoning. Reduce the heat and cook for 2 minutes. Set aside to cool completely.

3 Loosen the skin of the chickens then starting from the neck: push the fingers under the skin and lift it gently, being careful not to tear it. Continue right down to the opening. Insert the stuffing between the skin and the meat, putting any that is left into the inner cavity. Grill the chickens on a barbecue for 45 minutes–1 hour, turning them regularly to prevent the skin from burning.

This recipe is based on two of my favourite ingredients — chicken and mushrooms. I particularly recommend the mixture of button mushrooms and fresh shiitake, but dried black mushrooms (see page 3 of the glossary) may replace the latter. I chose to cook the chicken on the grill, but I could equally have chosen the method used for Roast Chicken with Ginger and Orange (page 96). However, grilling gives the chicken a slightly smoky taste, which is accentuated by the mushrooms. The basil adds a delicate aniseed (anise) touch to the whole dish. This recipe takes a little time to prepare and the ingredients are expensive, but for special occasions it is well worth it. You could spend the morning preparing this dish at your leisure and light the barbecue around midday. The leftovers will be delicious the following day and could even be taken on a picnic with a good bottle of red wine and a crusty baguette.

Chicken wings
roasted with peppers

Serves 4 • **preparation** 2 hours • **cooking** 20 minutes

750 g (1 lb 10 oz) chicken wings

Marinade
2 ancho chillies (chilies)
(large, dried, purplish-black
Mexican chillies. They are called
poblano chillies when fresh)
or 2 tablespoons Mexican
chilli powder or 2 ordinary
dried peppers
3 tablespoons Shaoxing
rice wine or dry sherry
2 tablespoons finely
chopped garlic
1 tablespoon light soy sauce
2 tablespoons bean sauce, puréed
freshly ground black pepper
fresh red chilli slices, to garnish

1 Remove the stalks and seeds from the ancho chillies and soak them in the rice wine for 45 minutes. Process the soaked chillies and rice wine in a blender together with the other marinade ingredients. Lay the chicken wings in a gratin dish, cover them with the marinade and leave to marinate for 1 hour.

2 Preheat the oven to 200°C (400°F, Gas Mark 6). Roast the chicken wings for 20 minutes, or until they are just nicely browned. Garnish with slices of chilli and serve.

It is a pity to underestimate chicken wings. It is true they require a certain manual dexterity with a knife and fork in order to access their delicate meat but, after all, this is a family dish, even a picnic one, so use your fingers!
You will note that, this time, I have gone to Mexico for inspiration and used the ancho chilli, which can be bought in food (grocery) stores specializing in South American products. If you can't find them, you could use the so-called Mexican spice mix, which generally contains a proportion of them in ground form. Failing that, use dried sweet peppers, since the ancho chilli is not particularly piquant. I have mixed these Mexican flavourings with Chinese ones to make a delicious marinade, which transforms the humble chicken wing into a dish fit for a king. While this is a simple dish to prepare, I can guarantee its success.

Young cockerel fried with spices

Serves 4 as an entrée • **preparation** 2 hours • **cooking** 12 minutes

2 young cockerels weighing about 450–500 g (1–1 lb 2 oz) each
750 ml (3 cups) groundnut (peanut) oil for deep-frying
60 g (generous ⅜ cup) flour
Garlic Mayonnaise with Sesame Seeds (page 226), to serve

Dry marinade
1 teaspoon coarse sea salt
1 teaspoon salt flavoured with Sichuan pepper (page 13 of glossary)
1 teaspoon freshly ground black pepper
2 teaspoons dried thyme

1 Cut each cockerel into quarters and wipe them on kitchen paper (paper towels). Mix all the ingredients for the marinade together in a bowl and rub the cockerel pieces all over with it, inside and out. Leave to marinate at room temperature for 2 hours.

2 Heat the groundnut oil in a deep-fat fryer or wok. Lightly flour the chicken pieces and shake off the excess. When the oil has reached about 180°C (350°F), deep-fry the cockerel pieces until they are nicely browned then drain on kitchen paper.

3 Just before serving, heat the oil to 190°C (375°F) and deep-fry the cockerel pieces again for 30 seconds. Drain on kitchen paper and serve with the Garlic Mayonnaise with Sesame Seeds.

The dry marinade, based on salt, pepper, salt flavoured with Sichuan pepper and thyme, gives the young cockerel the added flavour it needs. However, the delicacy of the meat is not changed in any way. The pieces are not coated in breadcrumbs, just floured and deep-fried in two stages; they come out of the oil light and golden, without excess fat. You could double or triple the proportions for this recipe for a special occasion. I like to accompany these chickens with Garlic Mayonnaise with Sesame Seeds (page 226).

Chicken
in two courses

In this recipe the two parts of the chicken — the legs and the breasts — which, with their different textures needing different treatments, each receive their due. In the case of the breasts I use the Sino-Japanese technique of poaching off the heat and, for the legs, the more universal one of grilling. The Chinese way of poaching is particularly good for the tender white meat of the chicken. It preserves the soft texture and delicate flavour. The meat is only briefly exposed to contact with the simmering water and the residual heat completes the cooking to perfection. This fits perfectly into the aromatic framework offered by the Sichuan pepper softened by the mildness of the butter and the Shaoxing rice wine. The butter is borrowed from the West: Asia makes greater use of oil and lard but, for all their excellent qualities, they cannot compete with butter in the matter of flavour.

The chicken legs are grilled because this method is best suited to their firmer flesh, which needs longer cooking. The spicy marinade — East–West variation of the French Persillade *— goes well with them. The marinade is lifted and reinforced by the addition of fresh coriander (cilantro) and orange zest to the traditional mixture of parsley and garlic. Their sweetness also counterbalances the slight smoky taste that results from grilling. These two chicken dishes are not only delicious; they bring out the contrast between the white and dark meats. Serve them as successive courses at a formal dinner party.*

1. Breast of chicken cooked with Shaoxing rice wine, butter and Sichuan pepper

Serves 4 • **preparation** 20 minutes • **cooking** 5 minutes

4 farm-raised boneless chicken breasts, skinned

salt and freshly ground black pepper

60 ml (4 tablespoons) Shaoxing rice wine or dry sherry

1 tablespoon whole Sichuan pepper

500 ml (generous 2 cups) Chicken Stock (page 218)

60 g (4½ tablespoons) cold butter, cut into small pieces

2 tablespoons chopped spring onions (scallions)

1 Lightly season the chicken breasts with salt and pepper then leave them to marinate for 20 minutes in the rice wine and Sichuan pepper.

2 In a sauté pan with a lid, bring the Chicken Stock to a simmer. Add the chicken breasts, together with the marinade. Simmer over a low heat for 5 minutes then remove from the heat and cover tightly. Leave to stand for 20 minutes.

3 Lift out the chicken breasts with a slotted spoon and keep them hot. Reduce the cooking liquor to two thirds, skimming it frequently. Off the heat, incorporate the butter a little at a time, whisking vigorously. Add the spring onions before serving. Serve the chicken breasts with their sauce.

2. Chicken legs marinated and grilled, Asian-style parsley vinaigrette

Serves 4 • **preparation** 20 minutes • **cooking** 40 minutes

4 whole chicken legs (thighs and drumsticks)

4 tablespoons finely chopped fresh flat-leaf parsley

4 tablespoons finely chopped fresh coriander (cilantro)

2 tablespoons finely chopped garlic

1 tablespoon grated orange zest

60 ml (4 tablespoons) olive oil

1 Bone the chicken legs in the following manner: hold them on a chopping (cutting) board, skin-side down. Using a thin-bladed knife, cut down the centre of the whole length of the leg. Detach the flesh by scraping it back from the bones with the knife blade, being careful to keep the meat in one piece.

2 Light the barbecue or preheat the grill (broiler). Place the parsley, coriander, garlic, orange zest and oil into a blender and process until a smooth cream-like consistency forms. Carefully coat the chicken legs and leave to marinate for 30–40 minutes at room temperature. Grill the chicken, skin-side down over the embers or under the grill. When that side is brown, turn the pieces over and grill the other side until the chicken is cooked thoroughly.

Pigeons 'lacquered' with honey

Serves 4 • **preparation** 10 minutes • **cooking** 35 minutes

4 pigeons weighing about 300–350 g (10½–12 oz) each

Marinade
1 tablespoon salt flavoured with Sichuan pepper (glossary, page 237)
1 tablespoon dried thyme
1 tablespoon spicy soy sauce
1 tablespoon Shaoxing rice wine or dry sherry
3 tablespoons honey
Corn Waffles with Spring Onions and Ginger (page 172)

1 Using a sharp knife, slit the pigeons down the back. Remove the backbone and rump bones. Break the breastbone and press the pigeons flat.

2 Mix the salt flavoured with Sichuan pepper and thyme together in a bowl and rub this inside the pigeons. In another bowl, mix the soy sauce, rice wine and honey together.

3 Place the pigeons, skin-side upwards in a single layer, in a high-sided dish. Using a pastry brush, brush the skin of the pigeons with the honey mixture and leave to marinate for 1 hour at room temperature. Preheat the oven to 230°C (450°F, Gas Mark 8).

4 Lay the pigeons, skin-side up, in a roasting tin (pan) or large gratin dish. Roast in the upper part of the oven for about 15 minutes.

5 At the end of this cooking time, reduce the oven temperature to 180°C (350°F, Gas Mark 4) and roast for a further 15–20 minutes, or until the pigeons are cooked but still a little pink. Remove them from the oven and leave to rest for 10 minutes. Cut each pigeon into 2 halves and serve each half on a corn waffle.

The pigeon, quite rightly, is something that is universally enjoyed. In this recipe it is roasted — a method which most cooks feel suits it best. Instead of basting the pigeons in the oven, this technique consists of 'lacquering' them with a sauce of Chinese origin, based on honey, Sichuan pepper, soy sauce and Shaoxing rice wine. The Chinese salt flavoured with Sichuan pepper and the dried thyme are strong notes, but the pigeons can easily stand up to them. All the aromas mingle admirably with the gamey flavour of the pigeon, backed up by the crispness of the lacquered skin and the incomparable creamy soft meat. This is a dish to savour slowly, meditatively. I like to serve it with Corn Waffles with Spring Onions and Ginger *(page 172), or on a portion of* Noodle Cake with Basil and Tomatoes *(page 157).*

Boned and stuffed quail

Serves 2–4 • **preparation** 30 minutes • **cooking** 10 minutes

4 quails weighing about 120 g
(4¼ oz) each, boned (see Boned
and Roasted Turkey, as shown
on page 94)
15 g (1 tablespoon) butter
1 teaspoon groundnut (peanut) oil
120 ml (½ cup) Chicken Stock
(page 218)

Stuffing
500 g (1 lb 2 oz) spinach (300 g
(10½ oz) trimmed and de-stalked)
15 g (1 tablespoon) butter
120 g (scant ⅔ cup)
soaked glutinous rice (as shown
on page 95)
1 teaspoon salt flavoured with
Sichuan pepper
(glossary, page 237)
120 ml (½ cup) Chicken Stock
(page 218)
2 tablespoons finely chopped
spring onions (scallions)
1 teaspoon sugar

1 To prepare the stuffing: wash the spinach in several changes of water to remove all traces of sand then drain. Melt the butter in a frying pan. Add the spinach, drained rice, the salt flavoured with Sichuan pepper, Chicken Stock, spring onions and sugar. Cook over a low heat for 10 minutes then leave to cool. Stuff the quails with this mixture and re-form them, keeping them in place with cocktail sticks (toothpicks).

2 In the same pan, heat the 15 g (1 tablespoon) butter and the groundnut oil together. Brown the quails on both sides then add the Chicken Stock and cook over a medium heat for 6–8 minutes, or until the quails are cooked. Lift them out with a slotted spoon and reduce the cooking juices by half. Pour this over the quails and serve.

In this recipe, the stuffing serves to heighten the delicate flavour of the quails without detracting from it. The spinach, for example, not only adds flavour and colour, but also helps to keep the meat moist. The glutinous rice adapts particularly well to this recipe: neutral in flavour, it takes on the taste of the other ingredients and softens the astringency of the spinach. It is not absolutely necessary to bone the quails, but it does add considerable refinement to the dish.

Stewed pigeon
with Chinese vegetables

Serves 2 • **preparation** 15 minutes • **cooking** 15 minutes

2 pigeons weighing about 450 g
(1 lb) each, quartered
salt and freshly ground black pepper
2 tablespoons groundnut (peanut) oil
30 g (1 oz) Chinese black mushrooms,
soaked and cleaned (see glossary,
page 232) or chopped button (white)
mushrooms
120 g (4¼ oz) peeled water chestnuts,
fresh or canned
250 g (9 oz) *bok choy*, washed,
trimmed and cut into pieces
5 cm (2 inches) long
250 g (9 oz) mangetout (snow peas),
topped, tailed (trimmed)
and de-stringed
2 tablespoons Shaoxing rice
wine or dry sherry
250 ml (generous 1 cup) Chicken
Stock (page 218)
1 tablespoon spicy soy sauce
1 tablespoon finely chopped chives,
plus a few whole chive lengths,
to garnish

1 > Season the pigeon quarters with salt and pepper. Heat the groundnut oil in a wok or large sauté pan and brown the pigeon pieces. Lift them out with a slotted and set aside.

2 In the wok, sauté the black mushrooms for 1 minute then add the water chestnuts, the *bok choy* and mangetout. Sauté everything for 1 minute then lift out and set aside.

3 Pour the rice wine, Chicken Stock and soy sauce into the wok. Add the pigeons and cook over a low heat for 10 minutes. Add the vegetables for just long enough to heat them through. Garnish with the chives and serve immediately.

The term 'to stew' conjures up an image of ingredients in a closed pan, seasoned and cooked slowly in a sauce, stock, butter or oil. This technique also exists in China using earthenware pots. The principle of stewing produces a homogenous dish in which all the elements keep their individual flavours. Here I have applied certain 'Nouvelle Cuisine' techniques to the venerable method of cooking in an earthenware pot.

Pigeon stuffed with cornbread

Serves 2–4 • **preparation** 15 minutes • **cooking** 40 minutes

2 pigeons weighing about 350 g (12 oz) each, boned and prepared according to the recipe for Roast Boned Turkey (page 94)

salt and freshly ground black pepper

½ loaf of Cornbread with Ginger and Chilli (next recipe – page 111)

120 ml (½ cup) milk

2 teaspoons light soy sauce

2 squares pig's caul (caul fat), about 23 × 23 cm (9 × 9 inches)

500 ml (generous 2 cups) Chicken Stock (page 218)

1 Season the pigeons inside and out with salt and pepper. Make the cornbread and let it get cold, then crumble it into a bowl and add the milk and soy sauce.

2 Preheat the oven to 240°C (475°F, Gas Mark 9). Stuff the pigeons with the soaked bread then wrap them in the pig's caul. Place them in a stainless steel or enamel roasting tin (pan) and roast for 10 minutes. Reduce the oven temperature to 200°C (400°F, Gas Mark 6) and leave to cook for a further 30 minutes.

3 Remove the pigeons from the roasting tin and pour off the fat, then pour the Chicken Stock into the tin and boil over a high heat until reduced by half. Transfer the sauce to a deep dish, add the pigeons and serve.

Maize, or corn, is a relatively recent addition to the Asian diet. My mother often cooked it and I enjoyed it prepared in many different ways, but particularly in the form of cornbread, the North American speciality that is more like cake than bread. I like its colour, texture and its delicate flavour, which goes well with a wide range of flavourings and preparations. I use it here to stuff the pigeons. For that I prepare it in advance and soak it in milk and soy sauce. To keep the flesh of the pigeons moist during cooking they are wrapped in pig's caul, a well-known technique in both Asia and the West. The fat melts gradually in the oven, basting the item as it roasts. The result is a rich, subtly spiced and very appetizing dish.

Cornbread with
ginger and chilli

Serves 6–8 • **preparation** 15 minutes • **cooking** 30 minutes

200 g (7 oz) fresh sweetcorn (corn) kernels from 1 or 2 cobs (ears)

2 tablespoons fresh red chilli (chili), de-seeded and finely chopped

2 tablespoons finely chopped fresh root ginger

2 tablespoons finely chopped spring onions (scallions)

salt and freshly ground black pepper

1 teaspoon baking powder

2 tablespoons sugar

150 g (¾ cup) corn semolina (polenta, not precooked)

60 g (4½ tablespoons) soft butter, plus a little to grease the tin (pan)

3 eggs, beaten

250 ml (generous 1 cup) full-fat (whole) milk

1 Preheat the oven to 200°C (400°F, Gas Mark 6). Mix the fresh sweetcorn, chilli, ginger and spring onions together in a bowl. Place the salt, pepper, baking powder, sugar and semolina in another bowl. Add the butter, eggs and milk and mix thoroughly. Add the sweetcorn mixture and incorporate carefully.

2 Grease a deep square 23-cm (9-inch) sandwich tin, pour in the mixture and bake in the oven for 30 minutes, at which time a wooden skewer inserted in the centre should come out clean.

3 Serve cut into squares, or use it as indicated in the previous recipe.

Duck served as two courses

Serves 4 • **preparation** 40 minutes • **cooking** 60 minutes

1 duck weighing about 1.5 kg
(3 lb 5 oz) (keep the carcass
to make stock)
2 teaspoons salt flavoured
with Sichuan pepper
(glossary, page 237)
Freshly ground black pepper

Marinade for the legs
2 tablespoons light soy sauce
1 tablespoon Shaoxing rice
wine or dry sherry
1 tablespoon spicy soy sauce

For the breasts
250 ml (generous 1 cup) Chicken
Stock (page 218)
1 teaspoon spicy soy sauce
1 teaspoon black Chinese vinegar
2 tablespoons butter

1 Remove the first duck breast by cutting along the breastbone and scraping the meat away from it to detach it. Remove the other one in the same way. Detach the legs.

2 Take the skin from the breasts and cut it across its width into strips about 5 cm (2 inches) long. Rub these strips with the salt flavoured with Sichuan pepper and the freshly ground black pepper.

3 In an earthenware or enamel gratin dish, mix the marinade ingredients together for the legs. Place the legs in the marinade and turn them so that they are well coated. Leave to marinate for 40 minutes.

4 Preheat the oven to 200°C (400°F, Gas Mark 6). Cook the duck legs, uncovered, in their marinade for 40 minutes.

5 Fry the strips of duck skin for 20 minutes over a low heat to render the fat and leave the skin crisp and browned. Lift this duck 'crackling' out with a slotted spoon and set aside.

6 Over a high heat, in the same pan, brown the duck breasts for 2 minutes on each side. Remove them from the pan and keep them hot. Pour off the fat from the pan and return the pan to a high heat. Pour in the Chicken Stock and reduce to about 60 ml (4 tablespoons). Add the soy sauce, black vinegar and butter and stir vigorously. Remove from the heat.

7 Slice the duck breasts diagonally across. Coat a serving dish with the sauce and lay the slices of duck breast on it. Serve the breasts first and the roasted legs afterwards.

This recipe was inspired by the classic Canard à la Rouennaise, *which is served in two stages.*

Braised duck

1 duck weighing about 1.5 kg
(3 lb 5 oz), quartered
salt and freshly ground
black pepper
750 ml (3 cups) Chicken Stock
(page 218)
2 tablespoons very finely chopped
fresh lemon grass
1 teaspoon chopped fresh
root ginger
2 tablespoons dried tomatoes,
chopped
1 tablespoon dried thyme
2 tablespoons Shaoxing rice wine
or dry sherry
2 tablespoons spicy soy sauce
1 tablespoon light soy sauce
3 tablespoons plum sauce
2 good fresh rosemary sprigs

1 Season the duck inside and out with salt and pepper.

2 Preheat the oven to 240°C (475°F, Gas Mark 9). Place the duck pieces on a grid in a large roasting tin (pan) and roast for 30 minutes, or until they are nicely browned. Transfer them to a large oval cast-iron casserole, add the rest of the ingredients and bring to a simmer over a medium heat. Cover the pan tightly and braise the duck for 40 minutes, or until it is tender. Remove from the heat, skim off the fat from the sauce and serve.

Braising is a method used equally often in Asia as in the West. Carried out in a covered pan over a low heat, it permits the flavours of the ingredients to merge gently while the process tenderizes them. More often than not, the items to be braised are first browned in oil or butter, but I have replaced this stage by a short time in the oven to sear the duck. As to the plum sauce, it is often used in braising sauces in Chinese dishes. As well as being easy to prepare, braised duck is an exceptionally good dish.

Peking duck 'lacquered' with orange

Serves 4–6 • **preparation** 15 minutes • **cooking** 1 heure 10 minutes

1 Barbary, Muscovy, Long Island
or Peking duck
salt and freshly ground
black pepper
250 ml (generous 1 cup)
fresh orange juice

Lacquer
1 litre (4 cups) water, plus 250 ml
(generous 1 cup) water
3 tablespoons spicy soy sauce
2 tablespoons honey
1 orange, cut into slices, to garnish

Sauce
2 tablespoons finely grated orange zest
250 ml (generous 1 cup) Chicken Stock
(page 218)
1 tablespoon Shaoxing rice wine or dry
sherry
½ teaspoon chopped fresh root ginger
1 tablespoon Grand Marnier
salt and freshly ground black pepper
2 tablespoons cold butter, cut into
small pieces

1 Season the duck inside and out with salt and pepper. Pour the orange juice into the duck cavity and close both ends with bamboo skewers, then tie them with string to ensure a perfect seal.

2 Place the ingredients for the lacquer except the 250 ml (generous 1 cup) water into a saucepan and bring to the boil. Remove the pan from the heat and pour this hot liquid over the duck several times. Leave the duck to cool completely in a cool, airy place for 5 hours, or 2 hours in front of a fan. When the duck is properly dried the skin should have the appearance of parchment.

3 Preheat the oven to 240°C (475°F, Gas Mark 9). Set the duck on a grid in a roasting tin (pan). Add the 250 ml (generous 1 cup) water and roast the duck for 20 minutes, then reduce the oven temperature to 200°C (400°F, Gas Mark 6) and roast for a further 40 minutes. Increase the oven temperature to 240°C (475°F, Gas Mark 9) and roast for a further 10 minutes.

4 Remove the duck from the oven and carefully pour the orange juice into a saucepan. Add the orange zest, Chicken Stock, Shaoxing rice wine, ginger, Grand Marnier and salt and pepper. Reduce the sauce by half over a high heat. Whisk in the butter and remove from the heat. Carve the duck and arrange it on a serving dish, garnished with the orange slices. Serve the sauce separately.

France was where I discovered that an orange sauce is delicious with duck. The affinity between these two ingredients struck me very forcibly. I think that the Chinese way of cooking duck is unrivalled, notably that of Peking duck, which inspired this recipe. I pour a specially prepared 'lacquer' repeatedly over the duck and leave it to dry for several hours.

Fricassee of chicken

Serves 4–6 • **preparation** 20 minutes • **cooking** 25 minutes

1 farm-reared chicken weighing about 1.25 kg (2 lb 12 oz)

2 litres (8½ cups) Chicken Stock (page 218)

3 medium carrots

250 g (9 oz) green asparagus

10 spring onions (scallions), washed and cut into 5 cm (2 inch) lengths

450 g (1 lb) red (bell) peppers, de-seeded and cut into strips 2.5 cm (1 inch) long

100 g (3½ oz) sugar snap peas, topped, tailed (trimmed) and de-stringed

50 g (1¼ oz) black mushrooms, soaked (see glossary, page 232)

30 g (2 tablespoons) butter

70 ml (4½ tablespoons) water

salt and freshly ground black pepper

Sauce

2 teaspoons finely chopped fresh root ginger

2 tablespoons finely chopped spring onions (scallions)

3 tablespoons finely chopped fresh coriander (cilantro)

2 tablespoons crème fraîche (or sour cream)

1 In a cast-iron casserole, bring the Chicken Stock to the boil and add the chicken. Cook for 20 minutes, skimming regularly. Remove from the heat, cover tightly and leave to poach for 1 hour.

2 During this time, cut the carrots diagonally into chunks and the green asparagus into 5 cm (2 inch) lengths and blanch in boiling salted water. (The carrots will need a little longer than the asparagus.) Refresh them in very cold water then drain and reserve with the other vegetables.

3 When the hour is finished, remove the chicken from the stock and skim off the fat. Reduce the cooking liquor by half over a high heat. Bone the chicken and set the meat aside.

4 Place all the vegetables (including the carrots and asparagus), butter, water, salt and pepper in a wok or large sauté pan and sauté for 3 minutes over a high heat. At the same time, add all the ingredients for the sauce to the reduced stock. Combine the chicken, sauce and vegetables, reheat briefly and serve.

This is a real Franco-Asian dish. The chicken is first poached in a Chinese marinade, which gives it succulence and tenderness. In China, this chicken dish would be served cold accompanied by a sauce, but here I have added blanched vegetables and a sauce copied from those that traditionally accompany chicken. The crème fraîche brings a final, smooth touch to a stew that is rich in flavours, colours and a variety of textures.

Quail, marinated and grilled

Serves 4 as an entrée • **preparation** 10 minutes • **cooking** 10–12 minutes

4 quails weighing about
100 g (3½ oz) each

Marinade
2 tablespoons light soy sauce
1 tablespoon Shaoxing rice
wine or dry sherry
1 tablespoon olive oil
salt and freshly ground
black pepper

1 Mix all the marinade ingredients together, add the quails and leave to marinate for 1 hour at room temperature.

2 Light the barbecue and when the embers have turned whitish, grill the quails, turning them halfway through cooking. The meat should remain pink in the centre. Leave to stand for 5 minutes before serving.

Other than enhancing the flavours, this method of cooking has the advantage of requiring very little preparation. Delicious food, such as these grilled quails, can be effortlessly produced. The secret of the recipe is in the deceptive simplicity of the marinade, which needs only a short time to impregnate the meat of the quail and enhance its natural delicacy. The quails can be eaten hot, as soon as they are cooked, or when cold, on a picnic, for example.

Creamed breast of chicken with red peppers and *bok choy*

Serves 4 • **preparation** 20 minutes • **cooking** 10 minutes

700 g (1 lb 9 oz) farm-reared chicken breast, skinned

2 tablespoons chopped spring onions (scallions)

salt and freshly ground black pepper

450 g (1 lb) *bok choy*, washed and drained

250 ml (generous 1 cup) Chicken Stock (page 218)

30 g (2 tablespoons) butter

450 g (1 lb) red (bell) peppers, de-seeded and cut into 5-cm (2-inch) strips

2 tablespoons crème fraîche (or sour cream)

1 Cut the chicken into strips 7 cm (2¾ inches) long and about 5–7 mm (¼ inch) wide. Place the chicken with the spring onions and salt and pepper in a bowl and mix together.

2 Cut off the base of the *bok choys*. Separate the stalks from the heart. Cut each of the stalks in half along its length then into 5 cm (2 inch) lengths. If the *bok choys* are large, peel the stalks. Cut the hearts diagonally in thin slices.

3 Heat the Chicken Stock with the butter in a saucepan. When it simmers add the chicken strips and cook over a low heat for 2 minutes then lift them out with a slotted spoon.

4 Pass the cooking liquor through a fine sieve (strainer) and return it to the saucepan, add the strips of peppers and cook for 2 minutes over a medium heat. Add the *bok choy* and cook for 1 minute until the leaves wilt.

5 Lift out the vegetables with a slotted spoon and set aside. Add the crème fraîche to the pan and reduce the liquid by half, adding more salt and pepper if needed. Add the chicken and the vegetables, reheat briefly and serve immediately.

The great virtue of chicken, in my opinion, lies in its relatively neutral flavour. The white meat, particularly, adapts itself to all forms of seasoning, which gives it their flavour without overshadowing its qualities. There is no doubt that the Chinese method of poaching off the heat is a spectacularly successful way of cooking it. In this recipe I have teamed it with bok choy; *a vegetable not unlike Swiss chard, though more delicate and sweeter. This vegetable combines with red peppers to pay homage to the chicken. The white meat is cut into strips, in the Asian manner, but instead of being sautéed it is first poached then cooked gently with the vegetables. The cream adds a Western touch at the end.*

Spatchcocked marinated pigeon with
Shaoxing rice wine sauce

Serves 2 • **preparation** 15 minutes • **cooking** 30 minutes

2 pigeons weighing about
350 g (12 oz) each
120 ml (½ cup) Shaoxing
rice wine or dry sherry
30 g (2 tablespoons) cold butter,
cut into small pieces

Marinade
1 tablespoon light soy sauce
1 tablespoon spicy soy sauce
2 tablespoons Shaoxing rice wine
or dry sherry
salt and freshly ground
black pepper
2 teaspoons sesame oil

1 Prepare the spatchcocked pigeons: open them with a cleaver removing the backbone. Flatten them with the palm of your hand. With the point of a knife make a small hole in each side of the wishbone (the high centre point of the sternum) and push the tips of the leg bones into them. This keeps the pigeons from distorting while roasting.

2 Mix all the ingredients together for the marinade and marinate the pigeons for 1 hour in a cast-iron casserole or an ovenproof gratin dish. Preheat the oven to 200°C (400°F, Gas Mark 6). Roast the pigeons for 30 minutes in their marinade.

3 Remove them from the dish and skim off the fat from the cooking juices. Place the dish on the heat and stir in 120 ml (½ cup) Shaoxing rice wine, scraping the base of the dish with a spatula to release the caramelized juices. Remove from the heat and whisk in the butter. Coat individual plates with a little of the sauce and place the pigeons on it. Serve the rest of the sauce separately.

In all human enterprises, simplicity is a great virtue. The problem is that, behind the scenes, things can be simpler — or more complicated — than they seem. This is why simplicity should not be a calculated factor but the product of discernment. I always seek simplicity in my cooking, but now it is arrived at by way of my experience and my own concept of what is simple. This dish, for example, is simple in my sense of the word, both in the recipe and the ingredients: a pigeon enhanced by a traditional Chinese marinade and simply roasted. To finish, just a little butter and Shaoxing rice wine, and simplicity becomes a royal treat. This recipe can also be made with young cockerels.

Chicken sautéed with sugar snap peas and water chestnuts

Serves 4 • **preparation** 10 minutes • **cooking** 5 minutes

500 g (1 lb 2 oz) chicken legs, skinned and boned
salt and freshly ground black pepper
2 teaspoons salt flavoured with Sichuan pepper (glossary, page 237)
1 tablespoon dried thyme
1 tablespoon groundnut (peanut) oil
2 tablespoons olive oil
500 g (1 lb 2 oz) sugar snap peas, topped and tailed (trimmed) and de-stringed if needed
250 g (9 oz) fresh water chestnuts, peeled and cut into 6–7 mm (¼ inch) thick slices
3 tablespoons water

1 Cut the chicken meat into strips 7.5 cm (3 inches) long and about 1.2 cm (½ inch) wide and mix them in a bowl with the salt, pepper, salt flavoured with Sichuan pepper and the thyme. Leave to marinate for 20 minutes.

2 Heat the groundnut oil in a wok or large sauté pan. Sauté the chicken strips for 3 minutes, the time needed to brown them. Lift them out with a slotted spoon then add the olive oil, sugar snap peas and water chestnuts to the wok and season with salt and pepper.

3 Sauté for 2 minutes then add the water and continue to cook over a high heat until the vegetables are cooked to your taste. Add the chicken for just long enough to heat it through and serve immediately.

This dish is not only easy to make, it seems to me to combine the very essence of Eastern and Western flavours. Sautéed in a wok, the ingredients retain all their qualities while cooking to perfection. The spices, the olive and groundnut oils and the thyme delicately flavour the chicken, while the sugar snap peas and the water chestnuts bring colour, flavour and texture, which delight the eye and the palate. This dish is marvellously balanced.

Marinated chicken
coated with sesame seeds

Serves 2–4 • **preparation** 10 minutes • **cooking** 10 minutes

500 g (1 lb 2 oz) chicken legs, skinned and boned
60 g (⅜ cup) flour
2 tablespoons toasted sesame seeds
1 egg, beaten
120 ml (½ cup) groundnut oil
fresh chive flowers, to garnish (optional)

Marinade
1 teaspoon salt
Freshly ground black pepper
1 tablespoon sesame paste or peanut butter
1 tablespoon chopped garlic
1 tablespoon sesame oil

1 Cut the chicken meat into strips 7.5 cm (3 inches) long and about 2.5 cm (1 inch) wide. Mix all the marinade ingredients together in a deep dish, add the chicken strips and leave to marinate for 1 hour.

2 In another deep dish, mix the flour and sesame seeds together. Dip the chicken pieces into the beaten egg then roll them in the flour and sesame mixture, shaking off any excess.

3 Heat the groundnut oil in a wok or large sauté pan and fry the chicken strips until they are golden on both sides. Serve, garnished with fresh chive flowers, if liked.

Fried chicken is very popular in Asia and it is also a North American speciality. I marinate the chicken in a spicy mixture based on sesame and garlic. The dominant flavour is that of the naturally powerful sesame. The garlic, too, loses its pungency in cooking. A simple and delicious dish.

Meat

Roast pork with Chinese spices

Apples (or pears) fried with ginger

Breast of pork in a barbecue sauce

Spiced pork chops

Roast rack of lamb marinated in a Chinese style

Grilled lamb marinated in rice wine and pomegranate juice

Confit of onions with ginger

Cubes of pork grilled on a barbecue, *satay* style

Round slices of shin of veal braised with spices

Fillet of beef poached with star anise and served with vegetables

Stuffed breast of veal

Grilled sirloin steak with oyster sauce and *bok choy*

Sautéed pork *paysanne*-style

Slow-cooked pork with star anise and cloves

Double lamb chops with leeks

Minced pork wrapped in pig's caul, with Chinese sausages

Braised oxtail with plum sauce

Veal sweetbreads braised in a chilli and bean paste sauce

Stuffed leg of lamb

Pork chops with *hoisin* sauce

Braised oxtail – my mother's recipe

'The line of customers moves slowly along the high marble counter, past the shelves and the trays where the cuts of meats are aligned, each with its name and price on a tag stuck into it. The vivid red of the beef precedes the light pink of the veal, the dull red of the lamb, the dark red of the pork. Vast ribs blaze up, round tournedos whose thickness is lined by a ribbon of lard, slender and agile counter-fillets, steaks armed with their invincible bone, massive rolled-roasts all lean, chunks for boiling with layers of fat and of red meat, roasts waiting for the string that will force them to enfold themselves; then the colours fade: veal escalopes, loin chops, pieces of shoulder and breast, cartilage; and then we enter the realm of legs and shoulders of lamb; farther on some white tripe glows, a liver glistens blackly...'

Italo Calvino, *Mr Palomar*

'Heaven sends us good meat, but the Devil sends cooks.'

David Garrick

When you make a comparative study of Asian and Western dietary practices, the differences jump out at you, particularly in regard to the place occupied by meat. In Asia, for a whole range of cultural, geographic and religious reasons, it is regarded as a secondary food. In China, meat is classed as one of those food items that 'help the rice go down'.

In the West, however, meat has long occupied a central position, even in the most frugal of diets. This concept could never have gained acceptance in the traditional Asian world but the situation is constantly evolving. Nowadays, in those Asian countries converted to a 'modern' way of life, meat is increasingly abundant and available; this is 'progress', we are told, and a response to consumer demand. There is surely an element of truth in that – even the Chinese of former days would certainly have been delighted to include more meat in their habitual diet, given the opportunity.

This cultural difference, however, in no way inhibits me in the creation of East–West dishes as I see them. All meat lends itself readily to the preparation of delicious dishes, sauces and soups, whatever their origin. All that is needed (as always) is a little care and imagination.

'The pig, roasted according to the book of rules, hath a fair sepulchre in the grateful stomach of the judicious epicure'.

Charles Lamb, *A Dissertation upon Roast Pig*

Pork

Pork is common in both East and West but in China, particularly, it has always played the role of 'steak'. It has been that nation's favourite meat for more than 70 centuries. All our domesticated pigs are descended from the European wild boar, which the Chinese were probably the first to tame and breed almost 5,000 years ago. They have, therefore, had plenty of time to form a sound opinion on pork and the many ways of cooking it.

And indeed, this marvellous animal is an integral part of the very fabric of Chinese culture. The ideogram for 'meat' and that for 'pork' are one and the same, and the ideogram for 'home' is a pig on a roof. Among religious practices, particularly in southern China, the highest sacrificial act is the immolation of a pig to the Gods. In the Cantonese liturgy this sacrifice takes the form of a 'golden pig', that is to say a pig roasted whole, coated or 'lacquered' with a solution of sugar and malt, which gives it a fine, red-gold colour – a lucky colour.

In addition, pork is very nutritious and is an excellent source of group B vitamins and mineral salts. Pig's liver is very rich in iron. If you need to watch your cholesterol, you should bear in mind that pork, unlike beef, is not marbled with fat and so its fat content can be easily trimmed away. Finally, pork is inexpensive. It can be served on any occasion, from a snack to a sophisticated dinner party.

'One sentiment does not exclude another: Mr. Palomar's mood as he stands in line in the butcher's shop is at once of restrained joy and of fear, desire and respect, egotistic concern and universal compassion, the mood that perhaps others express in prayer.'

Italo Calvino, *Mr Palomar*

Beef, veal and lamb

Beef and lamb are as familiar in the East as in the West. They both have a definite flavour, although lamb has more character.

There is little to say about beef. Its adaptability, its taste, the many ways in which it can be cooked, and its texture that varies according to the part of the carcass it is cut from, are well-known to all. One should, however, say a few words about veal. Veal was unknown in the Chinese culture of my childhood; in fact, in Asia as a whole, the idea of killing a calf without good reason makes no sense. The bovine species is too precious and scarcity too ever-present a threat for anyone to consider committing such an act. In Europe the situation is very different. The relative abundance of bovine stock encouraged the consumption of veal, especially during those periods when hay and grain were scarce; it was better to kill a calf than to leave it to die of hunger. In Europe – especially in France and Italy – veal is now readily available and immensely popular.

Personally, I have problems with veal, due no doubt to my Chinese upbringing. To begin with, veal has a very subtle flavour – too subtle, even. It has virtually no taste and the meat, if the animal was very young, is flabby. That of older veal resembles beef, but is totally devoid of character. In addition, special care is required when cooking it, since it has no fat whatsoever. Overcooked, veal becomes dry and tough, whereas when cooked for too short a period it has no flavour. When I was a student in France I often bought knuckle of veal instead of the more expensive beef. I soon found that I preferred the stronger flavour of braised veal knuckle to the tender but insipid veal used for frying. Braising is, in fact, the best method of cooking veal – the knuckle, at any rate, since the fibrous meat and tendons need stewing for a long time.

Roast lamb is well known in the West, the Middle East and India, but plays no part in the culinary traditions of China and Japan where, in any case, meat is rarely roasted, and goats and sheep are more common than lamb. In China, this type of meat is considered to have a very strong taste and smell, which accounts for the lack of enthusiasm for it. Significantly, several East Asian languages employ the same word for both sheep and goat, which is perhaps a reflection of this indifference to them as food. Be that as it may, young kid is tender and leaner, more delicately flavoured than lamb, but properly cooked lamb is a great treat, as the kitchens of Europe and America regularly demonstrate. I adore roast lamb but my taste for it originates from my Western heritage rather than my mother's cooking.

Roast pork
with Chinese spices

Serves 6–8 • **preparation** 2 hours 20 minutes • **cooking** 50 minutes

1 short pork loin with
bone in 1.8 kg (4 lb)
(ask the butcher to leave
the back fat)
3 tablespoons coarsely chopped
fresh sage leaves
2 tablespoons fresh marjoram,
chopped
6 garlic cloves, lightly crushed
but not peeled
2 tablespoons fresh orange zest,
cut into strips
1 tablespoon fresh lemon zest,
cut into strips
1 litre (4 cups) Chicken Stock
(page 218)
a few fresh coriander (cilantro)
sprigs, to garnish

Dry marinade
1 tablespoon five-spice powder
2 teaspoons freshly ground
black pepper
2 tablespoons coarse sea salt

1 Lay the pork loin in a roasting tin (pan). In a small bowl, mix the five-spice powder, pepper and salt together and rub into all surfaces of the pork. Next, rub in the herbs, garlic and citrus zest. Cover and leave to marinate for 2 hours in a cool place, or overnight in the refrigerator.

2 Preheat the oven to 230°C (450°F, Gas Mark 8). Roast the pork for 10 minutes, fat-side up. Reduce the oven temperature to 180°C (350°F, Gas Mark 4) and roast for 20 minutes. Remove the joint from the oven and leave to rest for 20 minutes. (It can be prepared in advance up to this stage.)

3 Bone the pork (keep the bones) and skim the fat from the cooking juices. Place the roasting tin over a high heat and stir in the Chicken Stock, scraping the base of the tin with a wooden spatula to dissolve the caramelized juices. Return the bones to the tin and cook over a low heat for 30 minutes. Skim off the fat once more and pass the cooking liquor through a chinois or fine sieve (strainer) into a saucepan. Reduce by half over a high heat and set aside.

4 One hour before serving, preheat the oven to 180°C (350°F, Gas Mark 4) and reheat the joint for 20–25 minutes. Remove from the oven and leave to rest for 20 minutes before carving. Fan the slices out on a serving dish and cover with the sauce. Garnish with sprigs of coriander and serve. Some fried apples (next recipe) would be perfect with this dish.

The orange and lemon zest give freshness and character to this marinade. In Asia the use of the strong, spicy flavours of dried citrus fruit peel is very widespread. The Western practice of using the zest of fresh fruits seems more appropriate in this instance. Plum and Apple Sauce *(page 224) is delicious with this dish. Any that is left could be served cold with* Ginger and Chive Mayonnaise *(page 223).*

Apples (or pears) fried with ginger

Serves 4–6 • **preparation** 15 minutes • **cooking** 2 minutes

750 g (1 lb 10 oz) Golden Delicious
apples or firm pears, peeled, cored
and cut into 5 mm (¼ inch) slices

juice of 1 lemon

30 g (2 tablespoons) butter

1 tablespoon extra virgin olive oil

2 teaspoons finely chopped fresh
root ginger

3 tablespoons finely chopped
spring onions (scallions)

3 tablespoons finely chopped
fresh coriander (cilantro)

salt and freshly ground
black pepper

1 In a bowl, mix the apple or pear slices with the lemon juice to keep them from discolouring. Heat the butter and oil in a wok or large sauté pan, add the ginger and sauté for 1 minute.

2 Next add the apples or pears and sauté for 1 minute. Lastly add the spring onions and coriander and sauté for a further 1 minute, then season with salt and pepper and serve.

Originally French, this recipe is given an Asian touch by the addition of ginger and spring onions. In Asia fruit is rarely cooked. It is eaten fresh or dried and sometimes poached in soups. Fresh fruit makes a good accompaniment for roasts; it balances the richness of the meat as well as, and sometimes better than, vegetables. Here the apples or pears are an excellent replacement for the traditional rice, pasta or potatoes.

Breast of pork in a
barbecue sauce

Serves 4–6 • **preparation** 15 minutes • **cooking** 2 hours 50 minutes

1.8 kg (4 lb) breast of pork,
cut into thick slices
salt and freshly ground
black pepper

Barbecue sauce
500 ml (generous 2 cups) Tomato
Concassé (page 221)
1 tablespoon olive oil
225 g (8 oz) onions,
coarsely chopped
1 tablespoon chopped
fresh root ginger
3 tablespoons chopped garlic
3 tablespoons *hoisin* sauce
1 tablespoon sesame oil
2 tablespoons spicy soy sauce
2 tablespoons chilli (chili)
bean paste
100 g (3½ oz) fresh kumquats
or mandarins, chopped
3 tablespoons sugar
2 tablespoons Shaoxing
rice wine or dry sherry
2 tablespoons light soy sauce

1 Preheat the oven to 120°C (250°F, Gas Mark 1/2). Season the pork slices on all sides with salt and pepper and arrange them in a gratin dish. Roast for 2 hours to melt the fat and tenderize the meat. Set the cooked meat aside on a plate.

2 During this time, place all the ingredients for the sauce in a saucepan. Bring to the boil and cook very gently for 45 minutes. Leave to cool then blend to a fine purée. This sauce can be made in advance and stored in the refrigerator.

3 To grill the pork slices, coat them all over with the sauce. Light the barbecue and when the embers have turned whitish, grill the meat, basting it from time to time with the rest of the sauce.

4 Cook for 5–10 minutes, depending on the thickness. Serve immediately.

The idea of grilling sliced breast of pork on a barbecue is undoubtedly a Western one. I now prefer it to the Chinese recipe, though I am very fond of that too. I invented a barbecue sauce based on Asian and Western condiments, which effectively supports the robust flavour of the breast of pork.

Spiced pork chops

Serves 2–4 • **preparation** 1 hour • **cooking** 3 minutes

4 pork chops from the fillet
end of the loin weighing
about 100 g (3½ oz) each
1 tablespoon olive oil
2 teaspoons salt flavoured
with Sichuan pepper
(glossary, page 237)
½ teaspoon coarse sea salt
1½ teaspoons rubbed fresh
thyme or 2 teaspoons
dried thyme

1 Brush the chops with olive oil. Mix the salt flavoured with Sichuan pepper, sea salt and thyme together in a bowl and sprinkle on both sides of the chops. Leave to rest for 1 hour.

2 Light the barbecue and when the embers have turned whitish, grill the chops. Turn them over halfway through cooking and remove them from the grill when they are firm to the touch. Serve immediately.

This dish, spicy and subtle at the same time, will give you a new slant on the humble pork chop. It can be easily prepared some time in advance. Accompanied by a green salad or a vegetable salad, it makes an excellent summer lunch. Serve it with Plum and Apple Sauce *(page 224).*

Roast rack of lamb
marinated in a Chinese style

Serves 4–6 • **preparation** 20 minutes • **cooking** 40 minutes

2 racks of lamb weighing about 750 g (1 lb 10 oz) each, skinned and trimmed of fat
salt and freshly ground black pepper
2 tablespoons groundnut (peanut) oil

Marinade
2 teaspoons black pepper
1½ tablespoons sesame oil
2 tablespoons toasted sesame seeds
1½ tablespoons sugar
2 tablespoons Dijon mustard
1 tablespoon light soy sauce
2 tablespoons spicy soy sauce
2 tablespoons finely chopped garlic
1 tablespoon coarse sea salt
1 tablespoon fresh sage or 3 tablespoons dried sage
120 ml (½ cup) Chicken Stock (page 218)
2 teaspoons sesame oil
2 teaspoons sesame paste
30 g (2 tablespoons) butter

1 Season the racks of lamb with salt and pepper. Heat the groundnut oil in a non-stick frying pan and brown the racks of lamb on all sides for 5 minutes. Remove them from the pan and leave to cool.

2 Mix all the marinade ingredients together in a small bowl and carefully coat the lamb all over with it, using a spatula. Leave to marinate for 1 hour.

3 Preheat the oven to 230°C (450°F, Gas Mark 8). Place the lamb in a roasting tin (pan). Moisten the sage leaves (fresh or dry) and strew them over the lamb. Reduce the oven temperature to 200°C (400°F, Gas Mark 6), cover the lamb with foil and roast for 30 minutes. If you want the lamb to brown, remove the foil for the last 5 minutes.

4 Remove the roasting tin from the oven, transfer the lamb to a carving board and leave to rest for 20 minutes.

5 During this time, pour off the fat from the tin. Place the roasting tin over a high heat and stir in the Chicken Stock, scraping the base of the tin with a wooden spatula to dissolve the caramelized juices. Next add the sesame oil, sesame paste and butter. Mix well.

6 Carve the lamb and place it on a serving plate and serve with the sauce handed round separately.

Despite its tenderness, the lamb stands up in a dignified manner to this spicy marinade.

Grilled lamb marinated in rice wine and pomegranate juice

Serves 4 • **preparation** 2 hours 20 minutes • **cooking** 45 minutes

1 kg (2 lb 4 oz) leg of lamb, boned but kept in 1 piece

Marinade
2 tablespoons chilli (chili) bean paste
2 tablespoons spicy soy sauce
1 tablespoon light soy sauce
1 tablespoon coarse sea salt
3 tablespoons finely chopped garlic
freshly ground black pepper
2 tablespoons olive oil
1 tablespoon sesame oil
3 tablespoons lemon juice
3 tablespoons pomegranate juice
2 tablespoons rubbed fresh thyme
2 tablespoons finely chopped fresh coriander (cilantro)

1 Mix all the marinade ingredients together in a large glass, porcelain or stainless steel bowl. Marinate the lamb in it for at least 2 hours at room temperature.

2 Light the barbecue and when the embers have turned whitish, grill the lamb for 45 minutes, turning it frequently. When cooked, leave the lamb to rest for 20 minutes on a board before carving it into thin slices. Reserve the cooking juices and serve them with the meat.

This recipe was suggested to me by my friend, Narsai David, an excellent chef of Syrian origin. Lamb plays a major role in the cuisine of his country. After enjoying many opportunities to taste his lamb-based dishes, I invented a recipe that reflects his style, but with a few added touches of my own devising. In this case, the fusion of East and West takes place via the Middle East.

Confit of onions
with ginger

Serves 4–6 • **preparation** 5 minutes • **cooking** 5 minutes

50 g (3½ tablespoons) butter

225 g (8 oz) red onions, finely sliced

100 g (3½ oz) shallots, finely sliced

2 tablespoons finely chopped fresh root ginger

250 ml (generous 1 cup) Chicken Stock (page 218)

2 tablespoons sugar

1 cinnamon stick

salt and freshly ground black pepper

1 Heat the butter in a medium sauté pan, add the onions and shallots and leave them to sweat until they are transparent. Add the rest of the ingredients and simmer over a low heat for 5 minutes.

2 Remove the cinnamon stick then reduce the mixture over a medium heat until all the liquid has evaporated. Serve warm or at room temperature.

Cubes of pork grilled on a barbecue, *satay* style

Serves 4–6 • **preparation** 1 hour 10 minutes • **cooking** 3–4 minutes

500 g (1 lb 2 oz) shoulder of pork, cut into 2.5 cm (1 inch) cubes

Marinade
2 teaspoons light soy sauce
1 tablespoon spicy soy sauce
1 tablespoon chilli (chili) bean paste
2 tablespoons sesame paste or peanut butter
1 tablespoon fresh marjoram
2 tablespoons Shaoxing rice wine or dry sherry
1 tablespoon lemon juice
salt and freshly ground black pepper
fresh herb sprigs, to garnish

1 Mix all the marinade ingredients together in a large bowl. Add the pork and stir well. Leave to marinate for 1 hour at room temperature or longer in the refrigerator. Thread the pork on to bamboo skewers.

2 Light the barbecue and when the embers have turned whitish, grill the pork skewers for 3–4 minutes on each side. Garnish with herb sprigs and serve immediately with, for example, the Confit of Onions with Ginger (page 135).

During my frequent stays in Asia, I always like to eat satay; *while it originated in Malaysia, it has been enthusiastically adopted by the whole of East Asia. The traditional marinade for satay is made with openuts, lemon grass, coconut, chilli and other spices. For this recipe I have substituted certain flavourings and used cubed pork.*

Round slices of shin of veal
braised with spices

Serves 4 • **preparation** 15 minutes • **cooking** 50 minutes

1½ tablespoons groundnut (peanut) oil

1.25 kg (2 lb 12 oz) knuckle of veal, cut into slices

3 tablespoons finely chopped onion

2 tablespoons finely chopped garlic

1 tablespoon finely chopped fresh root ginger

1 litre (4 cups) Chicken Stock (page 218)

1 tablespoon light soy sauce

2 tablespoons Madras curry powder

2 tablespoons Shaoxing rice wine or dry sherry

500 ml (generous 2 cups) Tomato Concassé (page 221)

salt and freshly ground black pepper

1 Heat the oil in a wok or large sauté pan and brown the slices of veal on both sides then transfer them to a cast-iron casserole and place the onion, garlic and ginger in the wok.

2 Sauté for 2 minutes then transfer these flavourings to the veal in the casserole. Add the rest of the ingredients, stir well and bring to the boil, cover, then reduce the heat and leave to simmer for about 45 minutes, or until the veal is very tender.

The knuckle of veal is braised here in a mixture of spices and seasonings, which heighten its delicate flavour without overpowering it. This is a good winter dish, a sort of Asian osso buco, subtle and strong tasting at the same time. Serve it very simply, with plain boiled rice and a salad. It is very good reheated too.

Fillet of beef poached with star anise and served with vegetables

Serves 6–8 • **preparation** 20 minutes • **cooking** 30 minutes

1.5 kg (3 lb 5 oz) beef fillet
(tenderloin)
2 litres (8½ cups) Chicken Stock
(page 218)
6 star anise
3 tablespoons spicy soy sauce
2 tablespoons pastis or anisette
salt and freshly ground
black pepper
450 g (1 lb) small new carrots,
scraped and blanched
2 bunches of spring onions
(scallions), peeled but left whole
Purée of Turnips and Parsnips
Flavoured with Ginger (page 183)

1 Tie the beef with string as for a roast, at 5 cm (2 inch) intervals. Put a final string around the length of the joint and secure firmly.

2 Place the Chicken Stock in a large casserole, add the star anise, soy sauce, pastis, salt and pepper and bring to simmering point, then cover and cook over a low heat for 15 minutes. Add the beef and barely simmer for 10 minutes then remove from the heat, cover and leave to stand for 1 hour.

3 Remove the meat from the casserole and drain, then wrap the beef in foil and keep hot. Bring the broth to the boil and add the vegetables. Cook for 2 minutes then lift them out with a slotted spoon. Strain the broth and reduce it according to your taste.

4 Carve the beef into slices and lay them in a serving dish, surrounded by the vegetables. Serve the broth in bowls with a little of the Purée of Turnips and Parsnips Flavoured with Ginger in the centre.

Here I have followed the French method of tying the beef and used it in conjunction with the Sino-Vietnamese beef broth flavoured with star anise. The heat of the barely simmering broth seals the surface of the fillet of beef, locking in all its flavour and juices. The slow poaching process acts like a marinade, flavouring the meat and reinforcing this flavour until it is perfectly cooked and still rare in the centre.

Stuffed breast of veal

Serves 4–6 • **preparation** 15 minutes • **cooking** 1 hour

1.5–1.8 kg (3 lb 5 oz –4 lb) breast of veal, boned and trimmed

2 tablespoons olive oil

2 tablespoons light soy sauce

2 teaspoons sesame oil

2 tablespoons finely chopped fresh root ginger

500 ml–1 litre (generous 2–4 cups) water

whole chive lengths, to garnish

Stuffing

1 tablespoon olive oil

450 g (1 lb) minced (ground) pork

2 tablespoons finely chopped shallots

100 g (3½ oz) leek (white only), finely chopped

100 g (3½ oz) carrot, cut into very small dice

100 g (3½ oz) parsnip, cut into very small dice

2 tablespoons dried tomatoes, finely chopped

salt and freshly ground black pepper

1 First prepare the stuffing. Heat the oil in a wok or large sauté pan and brown the pork. Add the other stuffing ingredients and stir over a low heat for 5 minutes. Leave to cool completely.

2 Using a very sharp small knife, make a slit in the thickest side of the veal, between the layers. Enlarge this opening with your fingers, pushing up the top layer, then spoon the stuffing into it and pack it well down. Sew up the opening with kitchen string.

3 Heat 2 tablespoons of olive oil in a large, cast-iron casserole and brown the veal all over. Add the soy sauce, sesame oil, ginger and 500 ml (generous 2 cups) water. Bring to simmering point then cover and braise over a low heat for 1 hour, or until the meat is tender, adding more water if necessary.

4 When the meat is cooked, transfer it to a dish and leave to rest for 20 minutes. Remove the string and carve it into slices, across the grain of the meat.

5 Reduce the cooking liquor slightly before pouring over the meat and serving, garnished with whole chive lengths.

Boned breast of veal does not have a great deal of eye-appeal but it is inexpensive and, when stuffed, makes excellent dishes. It generally comes in two parts: ask for the part nearest to the fillet, which is more regular in shape and easier to stuff. The braising liquor makes a delicious sauce, imbued with the flavour of the vegetables and Asian condiments.

Grilled sirloin steak with oyster sauce and *bok choy*

Serves 2–4 • **preparation** 5 minutes • **cooking** 15–20 minutes

2 sirloin steaks weighing about 450 g (1 lb) each
2 tablespoons sesame oil
salt and freshly ground black pepper
1 kg (2 lb 4 oz) *bok choy* prepared according to the instructions in the glossary (page 229)
2 tablespoons oyster sauce

1 Rub the steaks all over with sesame oil. Season with salt and pepper. Light the barbecue and when the embers have turned whitish, grill the steaks.

2 While the steaks are cooking, briefly blanch the *bok choy* in boiling salted water, drain and spread them on a serving plate.

3 When the steaks are ready, place them on a board and cut into slices 2.5 cm (1 inch) thick. Arrange these on the bed of *bok choy*, run a ribbon of oyster sauce around them and serve immediately.

This dish was one of the most popular specialities in the Chinese restaurant where I served my apprenticeship. The Chinese do eat beef but not in the form of steak, so the customers adored this cooking technique when applied to their familiar sirloin. There's no doubt it was a good way of crossing a cultural barrier.

Sautéed pork
paysanne-style

Serves 4–6 • **preparation** 15 minutes • **cooking** 40 minutes

1 kg (2 lb 4 oz) breast of pork, cut into 2.5 cm (1 inch) cubes (ask your butcher to do this)
1 tablespoon groundnut (peanut) oil
225 g (8 oz) leeks, finely chopped
225 g (8 oz) carrots, diagonally sliced
1 tablespoon sesame paste
2 tablespoons *hoisin* sauce
1 tablespoon rubbed fresh or dried thyme
salt and freshly ground black pepper
2 teaspoons palm sugar (jaggery) or candy sugar
120 ml (½ cup) Shaoxing rice wine or dry sherry
500 ml (generous 2 cups) Chicken Stock (page 218)
500 g (1 lb 2 oz) new potatoes, scraped

1 Blanch the pork cubes for 2 minutes in boiling water then lift them out with a slotted spoon and drain on kitchen paper (paper towels).

2 Heat the groundnut oil in a wok or large sauté pan and brown the meat. Add the leeks and sauté for 2 minutes.

3 Pour the contents of the wok into a large, cast-iron or earthenware casserole and add all the other ingredients except the potatoes. Cover and cook gently for 25 minutes then add the potatoes and cook for a further 15 minutes. Remove from the heat and skim off the fat from the surface.

4 Serve immediately or leave to cool completely and reheat it later.

This dish is one of my favourites out of all types of cooking. A simple concept, easy to prepare, solid, tasty and nice to look at, this is a peasant dish blessed by countless generations of appreciative palates. The recipe is based on the Western concept of browning then stewing, to which I have added a few well-chosen Asian ingredients. The palm sugar gives a sheen to the spicy sauce that the pork stands up to valiantly.

Slow-cooked pork with star anise and cloves

Serves 4–6 • **preparation** 15 minutes • **cooking** 50 minutes

1.8 kg (4 lb) best rib of pork, boned and cut into 5 cm (2 inch) cubes

1 tablespoon groundnut (peanut) oil

3 star anise

6 cloves

3 tablespoons finely chopped shallots

250 ml (generous 1 cup) Tomato Concassé (page 221)

3 tablespoons *hoisin* sauce

3 tablespoons spicy soy sauce

2 tablespoons light soy sauce

2 tablespoons plum sauce

400 ml (1¾ cups) medium or sweet white wine

500 ml (generous 2 cups) Chicken Stock (page 218)

225 g (8 oz) carrots

225 g (8 oz) parsnips

225 g (8 oz) turnips

salt and freshly ground black pepper

1 Blanch the pork cubes in boiling water for 2 minutes. Lift them out with a slotted spoon and drain on kitchen paper (paper towels).

2 Heat the groundnut oil in a wok or large sauté pan and brown the meat on all sides then transfer to a cast-iron or earthenware casserole. Add all the other ingredients except the vegetables, cover and cook gently for 45 minutes, or until the meat is tender.

3 Peel the vegetables and cut into small dice then blanch in boiling water for 1 minute.

4 Adjust the seasoning. Add the vegetables and simmer for a further 5–8 minutes. Skim the fat from the surface and serve.

Here I have taken one of my favourite cuts of pork, best rib, and marinated it in a mixture of Chinese condiments and Western flavourings. The vegetables are prepared in the Chinese style, but cut into small dice – a practice that derives more from the influence of European Nouvelle Cuisine than Asia. All the ingredients are combined in the final stage and simmered together. If you cannot find parsnips, replace them with diced celeriac (celery root).

Double lamb chops with leeks

Serves 2–3 • **preparation** 10 minutes • **cooking** 15 minutes

3 double lamb chops weighing about 375 g (13 oz) each

1½ tablespoons salt flavoured with Sichuan pepper (glossary, page 237)

1 tablespoon groundnut (peanut) oil

3 tablespoons finely chopped leek (white only)

2 tablespoons finely chopped garlic

2 tablespoons Shaoxing rice wine or dry sherry

3 tablespoons leeks, cut into fine julienne strips

250 ml (generous 1 cup) Chicken Stock (page 218)

15 g (1 tablespoon) butter

1   Gently rub the lamb chops with the salt flavoured with Sichuan pepper. Heat the groundnut oil in a wok or large sauté pan and brown the chops on both sides, then lift out with a slotted spoon.

2   Add the chopped leek and garlic and sauté for 30 seconds then add the rice wine, the leek julienne and the Chicken Stock. Cook over a high heat until the leeks are tender.

3   Reduce the heat, add the lamb chops and cook for 5 minutes, turning them frequently. Transfer them to a hot serving dish. Add the butter to the leeks left in the wok, mix well then coat the chops with this leek sauce and serve immediately.

The Chinese have no great enthusiasm for lamb, which is a pity because it is excellent when properly prepared and not overcooked. For this recipe I chose a delicate cut: double lamb chops, which are slices cut from the fillet end of a lamb saddle. Leeks are not without character, but the lamb more than holds its own; at all events, the garlic and Shaoxing rice wine and the salt flavoured with Sichuan pepper all come together to tame the rather powerful flavour of the meat.

Minced pork wrapped in pig's caul with Chinese sausages

Serves 6–8 • **preparation** 10 minutes • **cooking** 10 minutes

450 g (1 lb) lean minced (ground) pork
225 g (8 oz) Chinese, Vietnamese or Thai sausages (*lap xuang*, sausage with *mei kuei lu* or with lemon grass, etc.), skinned and cut into very small cubes (see glossary, page 229)
1 tablespoon rubbed fresh thyme
1 tablespoon fresh marjoram leaves, chopped
½ teaspoon ground cumin
salt and freshly ground black pepper
225 g (8 oz) pig's caul (caul fat)
a few fresh basil leaves

1 Mix the pork, chopped sausages, herbs, cumin, salt and pepper together in a bowl.

2 Cut the pig's caul into 15 squares about 13 cm (5 inches) each side. Lay out a square and place a few spoonfuls of the filling in the centre.

3 Add a basil leaf then fold in all the sides to make a neat 'crépinette' or flat sausage. Repeat this process until all the filling is used up.

4 In a large, non-stick sauté pan, brown the 'crépinettes' over a low heat for about 10 minutes. Serve immediately.

Armed with this recipe you should have no difficulty in making your own sausages. The word 'crépinette' comes from 'crépine' – the French term for pig's caul, which they are wrapped in. You can order it from your butcher. The filling is made up of pork and chopped Chinese sausages, with added herbs and spices. The result is a real treat.

Braised oxtail
with plum sauce

Serves 4–6 • **preparation** 15 minutes • **cooking** 2 hours 15 minutes

1.8 kg (4 lb) oxtail, cut into chunks

1 litre (4 cups) Chicken Stock (page 218)

3 tablespoons plum sauce

3 tablespoons lemon sauce

250 ml (generous 1 cup) Shaoxing rice wine or dry sherry

500 g (1 lb 2 oz) new potatoes, scraped

1 handful black Nice olives

1 Blanch the pieces of oxtail in boiling water for 10 minutes. Drain in a colander.

2 Place the oxtail, together with the Chicken Stock, plum sauce, lemon sauce and rice wine in a large, cast-iron or earthenware casserole.

3 Cover and cook very slowly for about 2 hours, or until the meat comes away easily from the bones. Skim off the surface fat, add the new potatoes and cook for a further 15 minutes. Add the olives and wait just long enough for them to heat through then serve.

Oxtail, which is considered a very choice cut in Asia, is somewhat neglected in the West, for reasons that are easy to understand. In the East, economic constraints mean that cheap cuts are appreciated. In the West, where meat is abundant, these tend to be looked down upon. This attitude is totally unjustified: oxtail, prepared with the care it deserves – braised slowly in a concentrated sauce – is a delectable dish.

Veal sweetbreads braised in a
chilli and bean paste sauce

Serves 4–6 • **preparation** 2 hours 20 minutes • **cooking** 45 minutes

1 kg (2 lb 4 oz) veal sweetbreads
1 tablespoon groundnut
(peanut) oil
1 tablespoon plain bean paste
2 tablespoons chilli (chili)
bean paste
3 tablespoons tomato
purée (paste)
salt and freshly ground
black pepper
500 ml (generous 2 cups)
Chicken Stock (page 218)
1 tablespoon sugar
225 g (8 oz) carrots, peeled and
cut into small dice
225 g (8 oz) turnips, peeled and
cut into small dice

1 The day before making this dish, wash the sweetbreads and leave them to soak in cold water for 2 hours. Next place them in a saucepan of cold water, bring slowly to the boil and blanch them for 2 minutes. Lift them out with a slotted spoon and drain on kitchen paper (paper towels). Skin them.

2 Line a gratin dish with a layer of kitchen paper. Lay the sweetbreads on it and cover with another layer of paper then another gratin dish or a small baking tray. Weigh this down with a few cans or jars of foodstuffs and leave overnight in the refrigerator.

3 The next day, cut the sweetbreads into pieces of about 5 cm (2 inches). Heat the groundnut oil in a cast-iron casserole and brown the sweetbreads. Add all the other ingredients, except the vegetables, bring to simmering point and cook for 30 minutes. Add the vegetables and cook for a further 15 minutes. Serve immediately.

Sweetbreads are not unknown in Chinese cuisine, but I never ate them as a child; Europe was where I discovered them. I particularly like the rich, soft texture and the relatively neutral flavour that lends itself to so many seasonings. Sweetbreads are not simple to prepare but the result is well worth the effort.

Stuffed leg of lamb

Serves 4–6 • **preparation** 15 minutes • **cooking** 1 hour

1 leg of lamb weighing about
2 kg (4 lb 8 oz), boned
2 teaspoons salt flavoured with
Sichuan pepper
(glossary, page 237)

Stuffing
120 g (4¼ oz) black mushrooms,
soaked and trimmed as stated in
glossary (page 232)
1 tablespoon olive oil
3 tablespoons dried tomatoes,
chopped with a knife
2 teaspoons finely chopped fresh
root ginger
2 tablespoons finely chopped
spring onions (scallions)
2 tablespoons finely chopped
fresh coriander (cilantro)

1 For the stuffing, coarsely chop the black mushrooms. Heat the olive oil in a frying pan and fry the mushrooms, the dried tomatoes, ginger, spring onions and coriander for 2 minutes then leave to cool.

2 Preheat the oven to 200°C (400°F, Gas Mark 6). Lay the lamb out flat, skin-side down, and cover with an even layer of stuffing. Roll the lamb up carefully and tie it with string, securing the string tightly. Lay the lamb in a gratin dish. Rub the joint with the salt flavoured with Sichuan pepper.

3 Roast the lamb in the oven for 20 minutes, then reduce the oven temperature to 180°C (350°F, Gas Mark 4) and roast the lamb for a further 1 hour. Remove from the oven and leave to rest for 20 minutes before carving it.

I think that the characteristic flavour of lamb is never better than when it is highlighted by ingredients that have as much character as the meat. They could be in a sauce, a stuffing or an accompaniment. Here I have made a stuffing, which completes and even enriches the flavour of the meat. You will enjoy this dish the day it is made, but the leftovers are just as delicious.

Pork chops with
hoisin sauce

Serves 4 • **preparation** 5 minutes • **cooking** 5–10 minutes

3 tablespoons *hoisin* sauce

1 kg (2 lb 4 oz) pork chops

1 teaspoon salt flavoured
with Sichuan pepper
(see glossary, page 237)

1 teaspoon cayenne pepper

1 teaspoon ground cumin

1 teaspoon fine salt

freshly ground black pepper

1 Spread the *hoisin* sauce on both sides of the chops, then coat them with the spices, mixed together, and season with the salt and pepper.

2 Light the barbecue and when the embers have turned whitish, grill the chops for 5–10 minutes on each side, depending on their thickness. Serve immediately.

There are days when nothing is more appealing than a simple, quickly prepared dish, such as a grilled pork chop. This is a treat that is made in a flash, and the satisfaction it gives is out of all proportion to the time spent on preparing it. A few Asian condiments, a little time in a marinade and off to the grill! That's all it involves.

Braised oxtail —
my mother's recipe

Serves 4–6 • **preparation** 10 minutes • **cooking** 2 hours 20 minutes

1 kg (2 lb 4 oz) oxtail, cut into chunks
1 litre (4 cups) Tomato Concassé (page 221)
1 tablespoon olive oil
1 tablespoon groundnut (peanut) oil
225 g (8 oz) onions, peeled and coarsely chopped
2 tablespoons finely chopped garlic
3 tablespoons plum sauce
2 tablespoons *hoisin* sauce
3 tablespoons Shaoxing rice wine or dry sherry
grated zest of 1 lemon
2 tablespoons light soy sauce
salt and freshly ground black pepper
450 g (1 lb) carrots
450 g (1 lb) turnips
450 g (1 lb) new potatoes
1 handful black Nice olives

1 Blanch the chunks of oxtail in boiling water for 10 minutes. Drain them carefully though a colander and dry on kitchen paper (paper towels). Mix the Tomato Concassé for a few moments then pass though a vegetable mill. Set aside.

2 Heat a cast-iron casserole over a medium heat. Add the olive and groundnut oils and brown the pieces of oxtail on all sides. Lift them out with a slotted spoon and pour off all but 1 tablespoon of oil from the casserole. Add the onions and garlic to the casserole and leave to sweat for a few minutes until the onion becomes translucent.

3 Add the oxtail, tomatoes, plum sauce, *hoisin* sauce, Shaoxing rice wine, lemon zest, soy sauce and salt and pepper. Bring to the boil then reduce the heat, cover and cook gently for about 2 hours, or until the meat comes easily away from the bones. Skim off the fat periodically.

4 Add the carrots, turnips and potatoes, peeled and cut into 2.5 cm (1 inch) rings. Cover and cook for a further 20 minutes, or until the oxtail is perfectly tender. Add the olives and wait until they heat through, skim off the fat one last time and serve immediately.

My mother — who to this day has never spoken a word of anything except Chinese — often prepared oxtail in this way, a judicious combination of Asian and Western flavours. All the influences come together to make this a delectable family dish, the perfect joining of two cultures.

Pasta, noodles and rice

Rice vermicelli Provençal style

Noodle cake with tomato and basil

Rice vermicelli with mushrooms and tomato-ginger sauce

Cannelloni with Chinese sausage

Ravioli with *bok choy* filling

Rice vermicelli 'Primavera'

Pasta with Chinese mushrooms and morels

Pasta with black beans and three kinds of tomato

Cantonese rice with duck

Pasta, noodles and rice

Whatever the origins of pasta, the Italians are now the self-proclaimed kings as far as the West is concerned. However, when it comes to pasta there is no longer any question of East and West. Gourmets from both hemispheres are in complete agreement about this. There are indeed as many varieties of pasta in Asia as in Italy, and it was the Chinese who invented the admirable rice noodle, which does not disintegrate in cooking, even in a very hot wok. Unlike pasta, made from wheat, rice noodles keep their shape when cooked in a sauce, which greatly improves the appearance and texture of certain dishes.

Fresh pasta forms an invaluable basis for all kinds of delicious dishes made with meat, vegetables, sauces, spices and condiments. Only rice has comparable properties and the following recipes are my way of paying homage to the admirable supporting role these popular foods play.

Rice vermicelli
Provençal style

Serves 4 • **preparation** 30 minutes • **cooking** 10 minutes

225 g (8 oz) dry rice vermicelli
3 tablespoons olive oil
3 dried red chillies
(chilies), halved
3 tablespoons finely
chopped garlic
1 tablespoon finely chopped
fresh root ginger
3 tablespoons finely
chopped shallots
225 g (8 oz) courgettes (zucchini),
cut into fine julienne strips
225 g (8 oz) red (bell) peppers,
de-seeded and cut into fine
julienne strips
2 tablespoons dried tomatoes,
cut into fine julienne strips
1 large handful basil leaves,
cut into fine julienne strips
salt and freshly ground
black pepper

1 Soak the rice vermicelli in a bowl of hot water for 30 minutes. Drain carefully through a sieve (strainer).

2 Heat a wok or large sauté pan, add the olive oil, chillies, garlic, ginger and shallots and brown well, stirring constantly, for 2 minutes. Add the vegetables and dried tomatoes and sauté for 3 minutes.

3 Finally, add the vermicelli and sauté for 5 minutes. Season with salt and pepper, add the basil and mix well. Serve hot or at room temperature.

Here I have used rice vermicelli, a common speciality in Thailand, Vietnam and southern China. They have an interesting texture — light and airy. Like all pasta made from rice flour, they benefit from the blandness of the basic ingredient, which makes them ideal in a wide variety of uses. For example, in this recipe the Mediterranean flavours rub shoulders with the Asian chilli.

Noodle cake with tomato and basil

Serves 4 • **preparation** 5 minutes • **cooking** 10 minutes

225 g (8 oz) fresh Chinese thin noodles made from wheat flour and eggs
3 tablespoons olive oil
1 large handful fresh Thai basil or ordinary basil, cut into fine julienne strips
250 ml (generous 1 cup) Tomato Concassé (page 221)
salt and freshly ground black pepper
3–4 tablespoons water

1 Blanch the noodles in a large saucepan of boiling water for 1 minute, then drain and set aside.

2 Heat the olive oil in a round, non-stick frying pan. Add half of the noodles, untangling them with chopsticks or a fork and forming them into a round cake. Spread the basil and Tomato Concassé over the cake and season with salt and pepper then cover with the rest of the noodles, pressing them firmly down. Reduce the heat and add a little more olive oil if necessary and possibly 1–2 tablespoons of water to moisten the noodles.

3 Fry for about 10 minutes, or until the bottom layer of noodles is crisp. Turn the cake over, add more olive oil and water and brown on the other side. Slide it out of the frying pan, cut into portions and serve.

This 'cake' is made up of two layers of egg noodles around a centre filling of basil (here used as a vegetable) and Tomato Concassé. Made in the Chinese way, the thin, fresh noodles are slowly fried in the pan, then turned over and fried on the other side, leaving the interior soft and creamy and offering a delicious contrast in textures.

Rice vermicelli with mushrooms and tomato-ginger sauce

Serves 4 • **preparation** 30 minutes • **cooking** 10 minutes

225 g (8 oz) dry rice vermicelli
2 tablespoons olive oil
3 tablespoons finely chopped shallots
225 g (8 oz) shiitake mushrooms, cleaned and trimmed of the hard end of the stalk
225 g (8 oz) fresh chanterelles, wiped with damp kitchen paper (paper towels)
salt and freshly ground black pepper
Tomato-ginger sauce (page 227)
3 tablespoons finely chopped spring onions (scallions), to garnish

1 Soak the rice vermicelli in a large bowl of hot water for 30 minutes. Drain through a sieve (strainer) and set aside.

2 Heat the olive oil in a wok or large sauté pan. Add the shallots and mushrooms and season with salt and pepper. Sauté over a high heat for 5 minutes, or until the water from the mushrooms has evaporated.

3 Add the Tomato-ginger sauce and the rice vermicelli and cook for 5 minutes, mixing constantly. When the noodles are cooked there should be very little moisture left in the pan. Garnish with the spring onions and serve hot or at room temperature.

This recipe is only possible because of the fortunate quality possessed by rice noodles of not disintegrating during the cooking process. Here they are prepared with two kinds of mushrooms — shiitake and chanterelles. The result is light and full of flavour, rich in textures and contrasting colours. It is another way of serving pasta.

Cannelloni
with Chinese sausage

Serves 6–8 • **preparation** 30 minutes • **cooking** 40 minutes

450 g (1 lb) dried cannelloni tubes
olive oil for oiling
double recipe of Tomato-ginger
sauce (page 227)
freshly grated Parmesan cheese

Stuffing
1 tablespoon garlic
2 teaspoons finely chopped fresh
root ginger
3 tablespoons spring onions
(scallions)
450 g (1 lb) minced (ground) pork
1 tablespoon olive oil
100 g (½ cup) glutinous rice,
soaked overnight in cold
water and drained
100 g (3½ oz) Chinese sausages,
cut into very small dice
2 tablespoons Shaoxing
rice wine or dry sherry
1 tablespoon light soy sauce
500 ml (generous 2 cups)
Chicken Stock (page 218)
salt and freshly ground
black pepper

1 To make the stuffing: finely chop the garlic, ginger and spring onion. Heat the olive oil in a wok or large sauté pan and brown the pork, stirring well. Pour off a little of the fat and add the rest of the stuffing ingredients. Cook over a low heat for 10 minutes, stirring frequently until nearly all the liquid has evaporated. Transfer to a bowl and leave to cool completely.

2 Cook the cannelloni tubes in plenty of boiling salted water, according to the packet (package) instructions. Drain and lay them on a clean cloth to cool completely. Preheat the oven to 200°C (400°F, Gas Mark 6).

3 Oil a large gratin dish with olive oil. Fill the cannelloni tubes with several spoons of the stuffing, continuing until it is all used. Arrange the cannelloni in the gratin dish as you make them. Cover with the Tomato-ginger sauce and sprinkle with Parmesan cheese. Cover with a sheet of foil and bake in the oven for 30 minutes. Remove the foil and brown for 10 minutes. Serve hot.

I was already an adult when I tasted my first cannelloni. It was in the South of France, at the home of Madame Taurines, my Franco-Italian adopted mother. She used to stuff them with a mixture of meat, spinach and Provençal herbs. I have eaten many cannelloni since, but none have ever tasted as good as those did.

Ravioli with *bok choy* filling

Serves 4–6 • **preparation** 15 minutes • **cooking** 5 minutes

450 g (1 lb) *bok choy* prepared according to the instructions on page 3 of the glossary
2 tablespoons olive oil
450 g (1 lb) minced (ground) pork
salt and freshly ground black pepper
2 tablespoons finely chopped fresh coriander (cilantro)
1 packet pastry squares for making Chinese ravioli (*wonton*)
2 tablespoons finely chopped chives
Tomato-ginger sauce (optional, page 227)
freshly grated Parmesan cheese, olive oil or butter (optional)

1 Finely chop the *bok choy*. In a wok or a large sauté pan heat the olive oil and brown the pork for 4 minutes, stirring well. Pour off any excess fat, add the *bok choy* and sauté for 2 minutes. Transfer to a bowl and leave to cool then add the salt, pepper and coriander and mix carefully.

2 Place about 1½ teaspoons of the filling in the centre of a *wonton* square. Moisten the edges with a pastry brush dipped in water, cover with a second square and press the borders to seal. Lay the ravioli on a lightly floured tray as you make them. Continue until all the filling is used up.

3 Bring a large saucepan of water to the boil. Add the ravioli, return to the boil and cook for 2 minutes. Lift the ravioli out with a slotted spoon and drain them well. Sprinkle with chives and serve with the Tomato-ginger sauce or simply as they are, with Parmesan cheese and olive oil or butter.

Bok choy has a delicious flavour similar to that of Swiss chard but sweeter. In this recipe, which was invented by a Franco-Italian friend, it is mixed with a little (ground) pork mince as the filling for the ravioli. The Chinese ravioli squares (wonton) are ideal for use in East–West cuisine as they can be filled with all manner of ingredients providing these go well together. This ravioli recipe is a perfect example.

Rice vermicelli 'Primavera'

Serves 4 • **preparation** 30 minutes • **cooking** 6 minutes

225 g (8 oz) rice vermicelli
225 g (8 oz) broccoli
225 g (8 oz) carrots, peeled and
cut into fine julienne strips
225 g (8 oz) thin green asparagus,
cut diagonally in 5 cm (2 inch)
lengths
2 tablespoons olive oil
1 tablespoon finely chopped garlic
2 tablespoons finely
chopped shallots
2 tablespoons finely chopped
spring onions (scallions)
1 tablespoon finely chopped
fresh root ginger
salt and freshly ground
black pepper
3 tablespoons Chicken Stock
(page 218)
225 g (8 oz) red or yellow
(bell) peppers, de-seeded and
cut into fine julienne strips
250 ml Tomato Concassé (page 221)
1 generous handful grated
Parmesan cheese

1 Soak the rice vermicelli in a large bowl of hot water for 30 minutes. Drain through a sieve (strainer) and set aside.

2 Cut the broccoli into florets and separate them from their stalks. Peel the stalks and cut them into thin slices and then into julienne strips. Blanch the broccoli, carrots and asparagus for 2 minutes in boiling salted water, drain and refresh them under cold running water. Drain again.

3 Heat the olive oil in a wok or large sauté pan. Add the garlic, shallots, spring onions and ginger. Sauté for 1 minute then add the rice vermicelli, salt and pepper and Chicken Stock and cook for a further 2 minutes.

4 Add the blanched vegetables, peppers and Tomato Concassé and cook over a high heat for a further 5 minutes. Transfer to a serving dish, sprinkle with Parmesan cheese and serve.

I have never found pasta heavy or indigestible. And I will go even further with this recipe, in which the Chinese rice noodles – in this case vermicelli – play the role of spaghetti in this great Italian classic. I offer this as proof that a light dish can be made even lighter.

Pasta with Chinese mushrooms and morels

Serves 4 • **preparation** 20 minutes • **cooking** 20 minutes

50 g (1¾ oz) Chinese black mushrooms
175 g (6 oz) morels, fresh or dried
3 tablespoons olive oil
2 tablespoons finely chopped garlic
3 tablespoons finely chopped shallots
salt and freshly ground black pepper
1 tablespoon spicy soy sauce
2 tablespoons single (light) cream
250 ml (generous 1 cup) Tomato Concassé (page 221)
225 g (8 oz) dried pasta (farfalle, fusilli, etc.)
freshly grated Parmesan cheese
3 tablespoons finely chopped chives, to garnish

1 Soak the black mushrooms in hot water for 20 minutes. Rinse and use your hands to squeeze the water from them. Remove the hard end of the stem and cut the mushrooms in half. If using dried morels, treat them in the same way, cutting them in half lengthways. If they are fresh, brush them lightly to rid them of any sand, then wash carefully and dry them well.

2 Heat the olive oil in a wok or large sauté pan and sweat the garlic and shallots until the shallots are translucent. Add the mushrooms, salt, pepper, soy sauce and cream and cook for 4 minutes. Finally, add the Tomato Concassé and cook for a further 2 minutes. Mix carefully then remove the pan from the heat and set aside.

3 Cook the pasta in a large saucepan of boiling salted water according to the packet instructions. Drain the pasta carefully and add to the mushroom sauce. Reheat gently then transfer to a deep serving dish, sprinkle with Parmesan cheese and garnish with chives. Serve immediately.

This is a simple but exquisite combination of flavours and textures, with a sauce impregnated with the woody, slightly smoky aromas of the mushrooms. The spices are in perfect harmony with the light pasta. The combination of pasta and mushrooms is often a successful one, and particularly so in this case.

Pasta with black beans and
three kinds of tomato

Serves 4–6 • **preparation** 15 minutes • **cooking** 5 minutes

350 g (12 oz) dried pasta (fusilli)

salt and freshly ground black pepper

3 tablespoons olive oil

2 tablespoons finely chopped fresh red chilli (chili)

3 tablespoons finely chopped dried tomatoes

3 tablespoons finely chopped shallots

3 tablespoons finely chopped spring onions (scallions)

1 tablespoon finely chopped fresh root ginger

2 tablespoons black beans

2 tablespoons coarsely chopped garlic

3 tablespoons tomato purée (paste)

2 teaspoons sugar

120 ml (½ cup) Chicken Stock (page 218)

250 ml (generous 1 cup) Tomato Concassé (page 221)

3 tablespoons finely chopped fresh basil

1 Cook the pasta in a large saucepan of boiling salted water according to the packet instructions, leaving them 'al dente' (still slightly firm to the bite). Drain and reserve.

2 Heat the olive oil in a wok or large sauté pan, add the chilli, garlic, dried tomatoes, shallots, spring onions, ginger, black beans and garlic and sauté for 2 minutes. Add the pasta and sauté for a further 2 minutes.

3 Add the tomato purée, sugar, Chicken Stock, Tomato Concassé and salt and pepper. Cook for 1 minute then finally add the basil and serve.

The practice of serving pasta 'al dente' requires a robust sauce and this one, backed by the chilli and the spicy black beans, is precisely what is needed. The tomato is an important factor in the texture, colour and flavour of this dish. The traditional east Asian aromatic trio – ginger, spring onions and garlic – is inseparable from black beans. In this recipe it fulfils its mission elegantly.

Cantonese rice
with duck

Serves 4–6 • **preparation** 15 minutes • **cooking** 5 minutes

1 tablespoon groundnut (peanut) oil

1 tablespoon olive oil

750 g (4¾ cups) cooked white rice

salt and freshly ground black pepper

1 teaspoon salt flavoured with Sichuan pepper (glossary, page 237)

250 g (9 oz) cooked duck or duck confit, boned and cut into julienne strips

100 g (3½ oz) mangetout, trimmed and cut into julienne strips

100 g (3½ oz) peeled water chestnuts, fresh or canned, cut into julienne strips

3 tablespoons finely chopped spring onions (scallions)

150 g (5¼ oz) cos (romaine) lettuce, finely shredded

1 tablespoon fresh red chilli (chili), de-seeded and cut into julienne strips

1 red (bell) pepper, de-seeded and cut into julienne strips

2 eggs, beaten

2 teaspoons sesame oil

1 Heat the groundnut and olive oils in a wok or large sauté pan. Add the cold cooked rice, salt, pepper and the salt flavoured with Sichuan pepper and sauté over a high heat for 2 minutes.

2 Add the duck, mangetout, water chestnuts and spring onions and sauté for 2 minutes. Add the lettuce, chilli and red peppers and sauté for a further 2 minutes.

3 Mix the eggs with the sesame oil and add to the contents of the wok. Stir and cook briefly, until the egg is just set, then adjust the seasoning and serve immediately.

Rice, though it is generally associated with Asia, is in fact a universal ingredient. Its growing popularity as a useful substitute for pasta, potatoes and bread is probably due to the ever-increasing enthusiasm for Asian cuisine. Cantonese rice, the traditional speciality that is no longer served nowadays, is prepared here with duck, which confers a touch of elegance.

Vegetables

Carrot purée with ginger

Braised parsnips

Corn waffles with spring onions and ginger

Potato purée with spring onions

Sugar snap peas sautéed with carrots

Vegetable spaghetti

Fresh corn and spring onion soufflé

Chinese ratatouille

Sweetcorn (corn)and spring onions grilled, with soy sauce flavoured butter

Mushrooms with rice wine

Purée of turnips and parsnips flavoured with ginger

Braised mushrooms 'East–West'

Green asparagus with soy sauce flavoured butter

Gratin of *bok choy* with glutinous rice

Water chestnut shoots sautéed with garlic

Summer vegetables sautéed with black Chinese vinegar

Buying vegetables in season is truly a pleasure. What a delight it is to choose them from the market stalls, testing their firmness and freshness and smell! Vegetables are much more than something that accompanies or complements the main ingredient of a meal; they are a complete food in themselves. One can, moreover, judge the quality and reliability of a restaurant by the freshness, flavour and succulence of the vegetables it serves and the care that has gone in to their preparation.

In this respect, it is generally acknowledged that *sautéing in a wok is the best way of cooking vegetables.* It preserves both their texture and nutritional properties and enhances their colour and flavour. The intense heat of the wok seals them, while constant stirring with a wooden spatula ensures that they cook evenly *without losing their vital minerals* (since there is no water to dissolve these). This is a method worthy of universal recognition and I warmly recommend it.

Vegetable purées are practically unknown in Chinese cooking as the texture of the ingredients – so essential to the country's gastronomy – is lost by this method. Purées are popular in the West, particularly in France, because their smooth nature is the perfect complement for the robust meat dishes that call for a plain accompaniment. The choice of a particular method of preparation should not be made in isolation; the context – colour, flavour, consistency and what is also to be served – must be taken into account too.

In Asia, stewed vegetables are more common than purées and I have included a dish of stewed parsnips among my recipes. The parsnip, though not particularly enjoyed in France and unknown in China, is one of my favourite vegetables when in season, because of its definite and strong flavour. As to carrots, they are popular in Asia, where the European carrot has replaced the sixteenth-century Asian variety, which was coarser and more fibrous. *I am proud to pay tribute to this loan from the West to Chinese cuisine!*

Potatoes and tomatoes

While potatoes are not a traditional part of the Asian diet, they have been known there for two centuries. I have always enjoyed them, particularly puréed or as my mother used to prepare them, mashed with a fork so that they retain some of their texture.

Of course, there were complaints about the lumps, but as far as my mother and I were concerned, she was merely manifesting the ancient Chinese respect for contrasting and balancing textures. As to the tomato, it originated neither in East nor West, but is a product of the New World. In Europe it has been used since the sixteenth century but it was only introduced to China 100 years ago. It has nevertheless transformed Asian cooking, as well as contributing a valuable source of vitamins and mineral salts.

Carrot purée with ginger

Serves 4 • **preparation** 2 minutes • **cooking** 5 minutes

500 g (1 lb 2 oz) carrots, peeled
and finely sliced
3 thin slices fresh root ginger
30 g (2 tablespoons) butter
2 tablespoons crème fraîche
(or sour cream)
salt and freshly ground
black pepper
2 tablespoons finely chopped
fresh coriander (cilantro)

1 Bring a saucepan of salted water to the boil. Add the carrots and ginger and boil for 5 minutes, or until the carrots are just cooked, then drain and discard the ginger.

2 Place the carrots in a food processor or vegetable mill and reduce them to a not-too-fine purée, gradually adding the butter and crème fraîche. Season with salt and pepper. Stir in the coriander just before serving.

Purées are not all intended to be baby food, as this recipe shows. It is important not to overprocess the carrots: turn the machine off when the purée is smooth without being too fine so as to leave it with a little texture. This purée reheats well and can be prepared up to two days in advance.

Braised parsnips

500 g (1 lb 2 oz) parsnips, peeled
and diagonally sliced
30 g (2 tablespoons) butter
250 ml (generous 1 cup) Chicken
Stock (page 218)
2 tablespoons crème fraîche
(or sour cream)
salt and freshly ground
black pepper
1 small handful fresh coriander
(cilantro) leaves

1 In a wok or a sauté pan, stew the parsnips together with the butter, Chicken Stock, crème fraîche and salt and pepper. After about 10 minutes, or when they are just cooked, increase the heat and add the coriander.

2 Cook for a further 5 minutes. The cooking liquor should have reduced by half. Serve immediately.

If you can't find parsnips, use this recipe for other root vegetables: bulbous chervil roots (this is quite rare), celeriac (celery root), turnips or simply carrots.

Corn waffles with
spring onions and ginger

Makes 8–10 waffles • **preparation** 15 minutes • **cooking** 5 minutes

500 ml (generous 2 cups) water

150 g (generous 1 cup) fine polenta (cornmeal)

1 teaspoon fine salt

2 egg whites

120 g (8½ tablespoons) melted butter

2 teaspoons sesame oil

1 egg yolk

60 g (⅜ cup) flour

1 teaspoon baking powder

180 ml (generous ¾ cup) milk

3 tablespoons finely chopped spring onions (scallions)

2 tablespoons finely chopped fresh root ginger

oil for oiling

fresh basil sprigs, to garnish

1 Bring the water to the boil in a small saucepan, add the polenta and salt and cook over a low heat for 5 minutes, stirring constantly. Leave to cool completely.

2 Whisk the egg whites in a clean dry bowl until stiff. Set aside until required.

3 Place the melted butter, sesame oil, egg yolk, flour, baking powder, milk, spring onions and ginger in a large bowl. Beat vigorously with an electric mixer or a balloon whisk, without overbeating the mixture. Stir in the cooked polenta then carefully fold in the egg whites with a flexible spatula.

4 Heat the waffle iron and oil it. Pour in a little batter and cook until it has gone crisp and golden brown. Repeat until all the batter is used. Keep the waffles hot in the oven until you are ready to serve them garnished with basil sprigs.

When well made, waffles are a treat. Light and crisp, they are universally adaptable and go with just about everything. Waffles made with polenta are particularly delicate and tasty, and their attractive colour is a bonus. In this recipe I have made them extra light and added a little ginger and spring onion.

Potato purée with
spring onions

Serves 4–6 • **preparation** 10 minutes • **cooking** 20 minutes

750 g (1 lb 10 oz) floury (mealy) potatoes, peeled and cut into 2.5 cm (1 inch) cubes
6 garlic cloves, peeled
225 g (1 cup) unsalted butter at room temperature
250 ml (generous 1 cup) single (light) cream
50 g (1¾ oz) spring onions (scallions), finely chopped
salt and freshly ground black pepper

1 Boil the potatoes and garlic in a large saucepan of salted water until they are cooked, about 15–20 minutes. Drain carefully then transfer them to a large mixing bowl.

2 Add the butter and half the cream then beat it with a whisk or a large fork until a smooth purée forms, adding the rest of the cream a little at a time.

3 Stir in the spring onions, season with salt and pepper and serve immediately.

Here I have added a little Asian touch — spring onions — to a good old family favourite. This purée is far from insipid — the cream and butter make it extra light and rich, and the spring onions bring a touch of crunchiness and added flavour.

Sugar snap peas
sautéed with carrots

Serves 4 • **preparation** 5 minutes • **cooking** 5 minutes

2 medium carrots, cut into
sticks about 5 cm (2 inches) long
and 5 mm (¼ inch) wide
20 g (1½ tablespoons) butter
1½ tablespoons finely chopped
shallots
500 g (1 lb 2 oz) sugar snap peas,
topped and tailed (trimmed)
and de-stringed
1–2 tablespoons water
salt and freshly ground
black pepper

1 Bring a saucepan of salted water to the boil and blanch the carrots for 2 minutes. Refresh them under cold running water then drain thoroughly.

2 Heat a wok or a sauté pan over a low heat and melt the butter. Add the shallots and sauté for 1 minute. Add the carrots and sugar snap peas and sauté over a higher heat for 1 minute. Add 1–2 tablespoons of water and cook until the vegetables are done to your taste. Season with salt and pepper and serve immediately.

Sugar snap peas, which used to be expensive and difficult to find, are becoming more and more available and their price is going steadily down. In China they are traditionally sautéed with soy sauce and rice wine, but I find this tends to spoil their delicate flavour. I prefer to serve them with a little chopped shallot, with butter, salt and pepper.

Vegetable spaghetti

Serves 4–6 • **preparation** 15 minutes • **cooking** 5 minutes

750 g (1 lb 10 oz) courgettes
(zucchini), cut into long
fine strips
1 tablespoon coarse sea salt
2 tablespoons olive oil
2 tablespoons groundnut
(peanut) oil
2 tablespoons sesame oil
4 garlic cloves, finely chopped
250 g (9 oz) thin green asparagus,
cut into 5 cm (2 inch) lengths
3 red or yellow (bell) peppers,
de-seeded and cut into
long fine strips
150 g (5¼ oz) fresh garden peas,
shelled and blanched (500 g
(1 lb 2 oz) in pod)
1 large handful fresh basil leaves,
cut into strips
salt and freshly ground
black pepper

1 Place the courgette strips in a sieve (strainer) and sprinkle with the sea salt. Leave to stand for 30 minutes then lay them on kitchen paper (paper towels) and wipe carefully. Set aside.

2 Heat the olive, groundnut and sesame oils together in a wok or large sauté pan. Add the garlic and fry for 30 seconds or until it colours slightly. Add the asparagus, peppers and peas and sauté over a high heat for 2 minutes. Add the basil leaves and leave them to wilt for a few moments then season with salt and pepper and serve.

The vegetables in this dish are cut into long strips rather like spaghetti then sautéed in a wok. The olive oil and the sesame oil, which both have low smoke points, are mixed with the groundnut oil to avoid overheating. This dish can be served hot or at room temperature as a salad with a little squeeze of lemon or a dash of sweet vinegar.

Fresh corn and
spring onion soufflé

Serves 4–6 • **preparation** 15 minutes • **cooking** 40 minutes

30 g (2 tablespoons) butter, plus extra for greasing
kernels from 5 or 6 corn-on-the-cobs (ears of fresh corn), about 350 g (12 oz), cut away with a sharp knife
4 finely chopped spring onions (scallions)
3 tablespoons single (light) cream
5 egg yolks
6 egg whites
salt and freshly ground black pepper
Tomato-ginger sauce (page 227), to serve

1 Melt the butter in a large frying pan and sauté the sweetcorn (corn) kernels and spring onions for 3 minutes. Set a little of this aside and blend the rest with the cream to a fine purée in a blender. Pour the purée into a mixing bowl and add the egg yolks, stirring constantly. Add the reserved sweetcorn.

2 Grease a 2 litre (8½ cup) charlotte mould and place it in the refrigerator. Preheat the oven to 230°C (450°F, Gas Mark 8). Whisk the egg whites with a pinch of salt until stiff.

3 Place some boiling water in a high-sided roasting tin (pan), set the mould in it and place in the oven.

4 Incorporate one quarter of the egg whites carefully into the sweetcorn mixture with a flexible spatula, then fold in the rest. Pour into the mould and turn the oven temperature down to 180°C (350°F, Gas Mark 4).

5 Bake for 40 minutes, or just until a wooden skewer inserted in the centre comes out clean. Serve immediately, accompanied by the Tomato-ginger sauce.

The sweetcorn dishes my mother used to make were always excellent and I have never forgotten how adaptable it is. For example, I had this idea of making a French-style soufflé from it. It contains no flour; the starch in the sweetcorn is sufficient to bind it together. The Tomato-ginger sauce (page 227) goes very well with it.

Chinese ratatouille

Serves 6 • **preparation** 20 minutes • **cooking** 10 minutes

225 g (8 oz) Chinese or ordinary
aubergines (eggplants)
225 g (8 oz) courgettes (zucchini)
salt and freshly ground
black pepper
100 g (3½ oz) small carrots
3 tablespoons olive oil
3 tablespoons coarsely
chopped garlic
2 tablespoons finely
chopped shallots
450 g (1 lb) sponge gourd
(or courgettes)
100 g (3½ oz) water chestnuts
(fresh or canned), peeled and sliced
250 ml (generous 1 cup)
Tomato Concassé (page 221)
2 tablespoons finely chopped
Chinese chives (or ordinary chives)
2 tablespoons finely
chopped chives
1 large handful fresh Thai basil
or ordinary basil leaves
120 ml (½ cup) Chicken Stock
(page 218)

1 Cut the aubergines and courgettes diagonally into slices, place them in a large colander and sprinkle them with 2 teaspoons fine salt. Leave to stand for 30 minutes then wipe them dry with kitchen paper (paper towels). Peel the carrots, blanch in boiling water and cut diagonally into slices.

2 Heat the olive oil in a wok or large sauté pan. Add the garlic and shallots and sauté for 2 minutes. Add the aubergines and courgettes, sponge gourd, carrots and water chestnuts.

3 Sauté for 2 minutes over a medium heat. Add the Tomato Concassé, the two types of chives, basil, salt and pepper and the Chicken Stock. Cover and simmer over a low heat for 15 minutes, or until all the vegetables are cooked. Serve hot or at room temperature, or even cold.

I chose Asian vegetables in a search for contrasting flavours, colours and textures. I used the classic ratatouille technique of cooking them all separately then bringing them all together briefly in a full-flavoured braising liquor. The result is well worth the effort of seeking out these exotic vegetables in prime condition, but if you can't find them, use other fresh vegetables in season.

Sweetcorn (corn) and spring onions grilled, with soy sauce flavoured butter

Serves 4 • **preparation** 2 minutes • **cooking** 5–8 minutes

100 g (7 tablespoons) butter

2 tablespoons spicy soy sauce

4 fresh corn-on-the-cobs (ears fresh corn), husked

8 spring onions (scallions), peeled and washed

1 Heat the butter and soy sauce gently in a small saucepan.

2 Light the barbecue and when the embers have turned whitish, grill the corn-on-the-cobs and spring onions.

3 Baste them regularly with the soy sauce and butter mixture, grilling them on all sides. They should take 5–8 minutes to cook. Serve piping hot.

Fresh corn-on-the-cob is a New World vegetable that has travelled to both East and West, though its arrival in the kitchens of Asia and Europe is relatively recent. In this recipe it is barbecued (grilled) rather than cooked by the more usual methods of sautéing or steaming. I have used spicy soy sauce in this recipe because its dark colour and strong taste goes better with corn than the saltier, less aromatic light soy sauce.

Braised mushrooms
'East–West'

Serves 4–6 • **preparation** 30 minutes • **cooking** 15 minutes

50 g (1¾ oz) dried ceps (cèpes)
(edible boletus)
50 g (1¾ oz) black Chinese
mushrooms, soaked and trimmed
according to instructions in
the glossary, page 232
2 tablespoons olive oil
3 tablespoons finely
chopped shallots
2 teaspoons finely chopped
fresh root ginger
450 g (1 lb) button (white)
mushrooms, cleaned and
finely sliced
2 tablespoons light soy sauce
2 tablespoons chopped chives
120 ml (½ cup) Chicken Stock
(page 218)
salt and freshly ground
black pepper

1 Place the ceps in a bowl, cover them with hot water and leave to soak for 30 minutes. Squeeze the water out of them using your hands. Cut the black mushrooms into wide strips.

2 Heat the olive oil in a medium-sized frying pan, add the shallots, ginger and then all the mushrooms and sauté for 5 minutes. Add the soy sauce, chives and Chicken Stock and cook over a medium heat for a further 10 minutes to completely reduce the liquid. Season with salt and pepper and serve.

Mushrooms are far too often relegated to a supporting role, but prepared with the care they deserve they are capable of occupying centre stage. Here I have combined two dried mushrooms – the Western cep and the black Chinese mushroom – and fresh mushrooms, and shown them off to advantage without detracting from their natural properties, thanks to a form of seasoning of my own devising.

Green asparagus with
soy sauce flavoured butter

Serves 2–4 • **preparation** 5 minutes • **cooking** 5 minutes

500 g (1 lb 2 oz) green asparagus, trimmed and washed
250 ml (generous 1 cup) water
1 teaspoon spicy soy sauce
30 g (2 tablespoons) butter
2 tablespoons single (light) cream
1 teaspoon toasted sesame seeds, to garnish

1 Peel the lower 5 cm (2 inches) of the asparagus stalks. Bring the water to the boil in a sauté pan and add the asparagus. Reduce the heat to medium and cook for 5 minutes. Lift them out with a slotted spoon and arrange in a hot dish.

2 Increase the heat to high and reduce the cooking water to 2 tablespoons.

3 Add the soy sauce, butter and cream. Beat well and remove from the heat. Pour this sauce over the asparagus and sprinkle with the toasted sesame seeds. Serve immediately.

The diet of the Southern Chinese is astonishingly varied, since the region is blessed with natural abundance. These are also people who enthusiastically adopt ingredients from elsewhere, such as this asparagus, which is now grown in great quantities in Taiwan. In Hong Kong, too, asparagus has made its debut in elegant cooking. Introduced in the 1970s, it now forms part of everyday fare in domestic kitchens as well as restaurants, where it is usually served boiled or sautéed.

Gratin of *bok choy* with glutinous rice

Serves 6–8 • **preparation** 20 minutes • **cooking** 40 minutes

225 g (1⅛ cups) glutinous rice
500 g (1 lb 2 oz) *bok choy*, prepared according to instructions in the glossary, page 229
1 tablespoon olive oil, plus extra for oiling
2 tablespoons finely chopped dried tomato
3 tablespoons finely chopped garlic
salt and freshly ground black pepper
250 ml (generous 1 cup) Chicken Stock (page 218)
6 eggs, beaten
3 tablespoons finely chopped fresh coriander (cilantro)
3 tablespoons freshly grated Parmesan cheese

1 Cover the glutinous rice with cold water and leave to soak overnight.

2 Blanch the *bok choy* for a few moments in boiling water then drain and chop them very small. Drain the rice.

3 Heat the olive oil in a wok or large sauté pan and sauté the dried tomatoes, garlic, rice and seasoning for 1 minute. Add the Chicken Stock and cook until all the liquid has evaporated. Leave to cool completely.

4 Preheat the oven to 180°C (350°F, Gas Mark 4). In a bowl, mix the cooked rice with the *bok choy*, eggs and coriander. Lightly oil a gratin dish and spread the mixture in it.

5 Sprinkle with the Parmesan cheese and cook in the oven for 40 minutes, or until a skewer inserted in the centre comes out clean. Serve hot, at room temperature, or even cold.

When I was a student in the south-east of France, my Franco-Italian adopted mother, Bruna Taurines, often prepared a delicious 'tian' (Provençal name for a kind of gratin dish, or something baked in it) made with rice and spinach or courgettes (zucchini). The smell from this dish as it came out of the oven promised a mouth-watering treat. I created this gratin dish, based on bok choy *and glutinous rice, as my tribute to her and the excellent cuisine of the Midi.*

Water chestnut shoots sautéed with garlic

Serves 2–4 • **preparation** 5 minutes • **cooking** 3 minutes

500 g (1 lb 2 oz) water chestnut shoots (or watercress or young spinach shoots)

1 tablespoon olive oil

1 tablespoon coarsely chopped garlic

salt

2 tablespoons chopped fresh basil

1 Trim the ends from the water chestnut shoots then wash them in plenty of water to eliminate any sand. Drain them thoroughly in a colander. Cut into 7–8 cm (2¾–3¼ inch) lengths.

2 Heat the olive oil in a wok or large sauté pan. Add the garlic with a little salt and sauté for 30 seconds. Add the water chestnut shoots and sauté for 1 minute. Add the basil, stir and serve.

Water chestnut shoots are extensively grown in tropical Asia, where there are numerous recipes for cooking them: soups, fritters, sautés, etc. Their flavour is like a blander version of spinach, but the main characteristics of this vegetable are its long, crisp stalks and small, tender leaves. It is important not to overcook them — as soon as the leaves have wilted they are ready. If they are unavailable, use watercress or young spinach shoots.

Summer vegetables sautéed with
black Chinese vinegar

Serves 4 • **preparation** 5 minutes • **cooking** 5 minutes

225 g (8 oz) yellow or red (bell) peppers, de-seeded
225 g (8 oz) small courgettes (zucchini)
salt and freshly ground black pepper
225 g (8 oz) young carrots
1 tablespoon groundnut (peanut) oil
1 tablespoon olive oil
3 garlic cloves, peeled and crushed
60 ml (4 tablespoons) Chicken Stock (page 218)
2 tablespoons black Chinese vinegar, or good-quality balsamic vinegar
2 tablespoons finely chopped spring onions (scallions), to garnish

1 Cut the peppers into fine strips and set aside. Cut the courgettes in half lengthways.

2 Bring a saucepan of salted water to the boil and blanch the carrots for 2 minutes. Drain and refresh under cold running water, then drain them carefully again.

3 Heat the groundnut and olive oils in a wok or large sauté pan over a medium heat. Add the garlic and sauté for 20 seconds then add the peppers, courgettes and carrots and sauté for 1 minute. Add the Chicken Stock and season with salt and pepper.

4 Cook for 3–5 minutes until the vegetables are tender. Add the vinegar, garnish with the chopped spring onions and serve immediately.

A dish of young summer vegetables, simply sautéed, is one of the great pleasures of the summer season. A touch of slightly sweet, mildly acidic black vinegar is just enough to bring out the flavours. Black Chinese vinegar is not unlike balsamic vinegar (which can be used as a substitute for it) both in flavour and the way it is made. Its effect is both comforting and stimulating at the same time.

Desserts

Mandarin sorbet

Almond madeleines

Coconut cream

Lychee sorbet with raspberry coulis

Ginger and blood orange sorbet

Cold melon and coconut soup

Small baked custards with orange and ginger

Baked apples with lemon grass

Warm peach compote with basil

Fresh water chestnuts and rum butter

Crème brulée flavoured with ginger

Almond cream

Lemon tart

Mango ice cream with crystallized ginger

'Dost thou think, because thou art virtuous, there shall be no more cakes and ale?'

William Shakespeare, *Twelfth Night.*

Kipling was mistaken when he wrote 'East is East and West is West, and never the twain shall meet,' but he wasn't too far wrong when it comes to desserts. In the West, dessert is the grand finale to a meal constructed like a symphony concert. Nothing of the sort happens in Asia, particularly in China and Japan, where sweet dishes don't come at the end of a meal, nor indeed do they form any part of its structure. The Japanese prefer the more discreet offering of fresh fruit before leaving table. As to the Chinese, they expect a meal to be sufficiently satisfying in itself, which is why – except in the case of a formal banquet – they do not follow it with a dessert. In Asia, sweet dishes are generally based on fruit or sweetened vegetables (beans, corn, soya, etc.) and either eaten outside mealtimes or between courses at a festive meal to refresh the palate. In Vietnam sweet soups are sometimes served as an accompaniment to savoury dishes.

Some *dim sum* – popular small dishes in Southern China – are sweet, but that does not make them desserts. They are snacks, with flavours that can range from very salty or very spicy to bland or sweet, but they are not served in any particular order in the course of the meal.

Asian cuisine has been very fortunate; refined white sugar was not introduced there until near the end of the nineteenth century, and more interesting sweetening agents, such as palm sugar (jaggery), unrefined cane sugar and honey are still currently in use there. Unfortunately the Asian diet, too, is now under attack from this ersatz industrial sugar, which destroys the taste buds while stuffing us full of calories that have no nutritional value.

Since desserts are an unavoidable fact of culinary life in Europe, I have done my best in the recipes that follow to combine various fruits, spices, flavourings, creams and sugars to bring out the essence of Eastern and Western sweetmeats.

Coconut cream

Makes 4–6 • **preparation** 10 minutes

1.5 litres (6 cups) canned
coconut milk
6 tablespoons sugar
2 large egg yolks
250 ml (generous 1 cup)
unsweetened whipping cream
a few sliced fruits or red berries,
to decorate

1 Place the coconut milk in a saucepan, add 3 tablespoons of sugar and leave to simmer for 5 minutes.

2 In a mixing bowl, beat the egg yolks with 2 tablespoons of sugar. Remove the coconut milk from the heat and very slowly pour it in a thin stream on to the egg and sugar mixture, whisking vigorously all the time. Return the mixture to the saucepan and heat gently, stirring constantly with a wooden spoon, until the cream thickens sufficiently to coat the back of the spoon. Don't allow it to boil. Set aside to cool completely.

3 Place the cream and the rest of the sugar in a bowl and whisk until just thickened then very carefully fold into the coconut mixture.

4 Store the cream in the refrigerator. Just before serving, stir, transfer to individual dishes or even fresh coconut halves and decorate with slices of fresh fruit or red berries.

This is an Asian variation on crème anglaise (basic custard sauce). It can be prepared several hours in advance. Stir it carefully before serving it accompanied by fresh fruit or red berries, whichever takes your fancy.

Lychee sorbet with
raspberry coulis

Serves 4 • **preparation** 15 minutes

Lychee sorbet

1 kg (2 lb 4 oz) fresh lychees
(litchis), peeled and stoned
(pitted) (reserve the juice)
170 g (generous ¾ cup) sugar
60 ml (4 tablespoons)
fresh orange juice

Raspberry coulis

250 g (9 oz) fresh raspberries
55 g (generous ¼ cup) sugar

To decorate

fresh fruit, such as raspberries
and lychees
fresh bay leaves (optional)

1 Purée the lychees in a blender or food processor then add the sugar and orange juice. Freeze the mixture in an ice cream maker, according to the manufacturer's instructions.

2 If you don't have an ice cream machine, you can pour the mixture into metal ice cube trays with their separators removed, or any similar shallow, freezerproof container. Every 30 minutes, stir the mixture with a fork to prevent ice crystals from forming.

3 To make the coulis, purée the raspberries in a blender, pass through a sieve (strainer) into a bowl and add the sugar. Store in the refrigerator until needed.

4 To serve, pour some raspberry coulis into each dish then place a ball – or a log shape – of sorbet in the centre and decorate with fresh fruit and bay leaves, if liked.

Lychees, originally from South-east China, are the favourite fruit of the Chinese. They are available in cans, but if you can manage to find good fresh lychees you will come to understand the words of the venerable Shen Fu, who said, 'The flavour of the lychees of Canton was one of the great pleasures of my life.' The combination of this jewel among Asian fruits and the pearl of Western fruits, the raspberry, has the same effect.

Ginger and blood orange sorbet

Makes about 1 litre (4 cups) • **preparation** 15 minutes

1 litre (4 cups) fresh juice from
blood oranges
115 g (¾ cup) sugar
2 tablespoons finely chopped
crystallized (candied) ginger

1 Mix all the ingredients together in a bowl until the sugar has completely dissolved. Freeze the mixture in an ice cream maker, according to the manufacturer's instructions.

2 If you don't have an ice cream machine you can pour the mixture into metal ice cube trays with their separators removed, or any similar shallow, freezerproof container. Every 30 minutes, stir the mixture with a fork to prevent ice crystals from forming.

The Chinese adore oranges and have many varieties of them but blood oranges are unknown there. Imported from Sicily or North Africa, they are very popular in France. The season for them is very short — only from January to March. I took inspiration from the French citrus sorbets and added an ingredient much appreciated by the Chinese — crystallized ginger.

Cold melon and coconut soup

Serves 6 • **preparation** 20 minutes

meat from 1 large fresh coconut (400 g [14 oz] shelled), or use 1.2 litres (5 cups) coconut milk, canned or in a carton
500 ml (generous 2 cups) single (light) cream
250 ml (generous 1 cup) skimmed (skim) milk
5 tablespoons sugar
2 very ripe Cantaloupe melons, cut in half and de-seeded

1 If you are using fresh coconut meat, cut it into small dice and place it in a saucepan with its own milk. Add the cream and skimmed milk and cook gently for 10 minutes. Leave it to cool, then place it in a food processor and blend at high speed for 1 minute. Leave to rest for 15 minutes then strain the liquid from the saucepan through a fine sieve (strainer), crushing the pulp with a wooden spoon to express as much liquid as possible. If you are not using fresh coconut meat, then omit this step.

2 Add 3 tablespoons sugar to the coconut milk, bring to simmering point and cook gently over a low heat for 10 minutes. Leave to cool completely.

3 Using a melon ball scoop, form melon balls weighing a total of around 200 g (7 oz) from the melons and set aside. Scoop out the rest of the flesh from the melons and purée it in a blender. Mix with the remaining 2 tablespoons of sugar and add to the cooled coconut milk.

4 Mix carefully, pour into a soup tureen and serve decorated with the reserved melon balls.

I got the idea for his recipe after tasting a cold soup based on tapioca and coconut milk in the Sichuan restaurant in Hong Kong. I left out the tapioca and added milk and cream. Coconut milk and melons are made for each other; adjust the amount of sugar to suit your own taste.

Small baked custards with orange and ginger

Serves 6 • **preparation** 10 minutes • **cooking** 35 minutes

6 eggs

120 g (scant ²⁄₃ cup) sugar

250 ml (generous 1 cup) single (light) cream

1 pinch salt

15 g (1 tablespoon) melted butter, plus extra for greasing

1 tablespoon finely chopped fresh root ginger

1 tablespoon fresh lemon juice

3 medium oranges, peeled with a sharp knife to remove all the pith and inner skin, and cut into segments

Raspberry Coulis (page 198)

3 tablespoons grated orange zest, to decorate

1 Preheat the oven to 180°C (350°F, Gas Mark 4). Whisk the eggs, sugar, cream, salt, butter, ginger and lemon juice together in a large bowl.

2 Grease a gratin dish or individual ramekins with butter and pour in the mixture. Arrange the peeled orange segments on the top then cover the ramekins with a sheet of foil and bake in the oven for 35 minutes, or until a skewer inserted in the centre comes out clean.

3 To serve, coat dessert plates with a few spoonfuls of the Raspberry Coulis. Take the creams out of the ramekins and place one in the centre of each plate (or a spoonful, if you made a single large one) and decorate with the orange zest.

I got the inspiration for this dessert from a very memorable day when I got up at 4 am and travelled from Paris to Crissier, in Switzerland, home of the great chef Freddy Girardet. It was a very worthwhile trip; the meal was a delight. I was particularly seduced by the dessert, a gratin of oranges 'Madame France'. Here, I have recaptured the recipe and added a Chinese note — a touch of ginger.

Baked apples with lemon grass

Serves 4 • **preparation** 10 minutes • **cooking** 30 minutes

750 g (1 lb 10 oz) Golden Delicious apples, peeled and cored, cut in half then into 5 mm (¼ inch) slices
50 g (¼ cup) palm sugar (jaggery), candy sugar or ordinary sugar
2 tablespoons finely chopped lemon grass
1 vanilla pod (bean), slit lengthways into 4
lemon grass stalks, to decorate
crème fraîche (or sour cream), to serve

1 Preheat the oven to 200°C/400°F/ Gas Mark 6. Cut 4 sheets of foil 25 cm (10 inches) square and place one quarter of the apple slices on each. Add a quarter of the sugar and chopped lemon grass, then a quarter of the vanilla pod.

2 Seal the parcels, lay them on a baking sheet and bake in the oven for 30 minutes.

3 Take them to the table, still sealed, on individual plates and let each guest open his own. Decorate with lemon grass stalks and serve with a bowl of crème fraîche on the side.

The vast range of desserts and pastries made with apples were invented in the cool northern regions of Europe and America: tarts, compotes, jelly, baked apples… In Asia apples are generally eaten raw or added to soups. Here I took the traditional baked apple and gave it an Asian twist with the lemon grass. The crème fraîche makes for a softer, richer combination.

Warm peach compote with basil

Serves 4 • **preparation** 10 minutes • **cooking** 5 minutes

115 g (½ cup) sugar

250 ml (generous 1 cup) water

1 kg (2 lb 4 oz) slightly firm peaches, peeled, stoned (pitted) and sliced

1 vanilla pod (bean)

60 g (4½ tablespoons) cold butter, cut into small pieces

1 small handful fresh basil leaves

1 Place the sugar and water in a frying pan and heat until the sugar dissolves completely. Add the peach slices and vanilla pod and simmer for 2 minutes.

2 Remove the vanilla pod and incorporate the butter, a little at a time, whisking constantly. Finally add the basil leaves. Leave on the heat until the leaves wilt then serve immediately.

Peaches, yes, fine. But with basil? In east Asia, star anise, with its hints of liquorice, is as likely to be used in sweet dishes as in savoury. I've followed the logic of this here and used basil — the 'royal herb' that graces so many savoury dishes. It is a good way of using peaches that are still slightly unripe.

Fresh water chestnuts
and rum butter

Serves 4 • **preparation** 2 minutes • **cooking** 5 minutes

225 g (8 oz) fresh water
chestnuts, peeled and sliced

2 tablespoons sugar

60 ml (4 tablespoons) lemon juice

60 ml (4 tablespoons) rum

30 g (2 tablespoons) butter

1 Place the water chestnuts in a frying pan with the water, sugar and lemon juice and stew over a low heat for 5 minutes.

2 Increase the heat to high and add the rum and the butter. Set it alight and when the flames have died down, reduce the juices to a syrupy consistency. Serve immediately.

In the Far East, fresh water chestnuts are considered a great delicacy with their crunchy texture and sweet, nutty flavour. They can be bought from stalls in the street. You can also find them caramelized or bottled in sugar syrup. Do make the effort to find fresh water chestnuts in Asian food outlets, rather than buying canned ones.

Crème brulée
flavoured with ginger

Serves 4–6 • **preparation** 10 minutes • **cooking** 30 minutes

15 g (1 tablespoon) butter
2 teaspoons finely chopped
fresh root ginger
3 tablespoons caster
(superfine) sugar
500 ml (generous 2 cups)
whipping cream
4 egg yolks
2 tablespoons soft brown sugar

1 Preheat the oven to 230°C (450°F, Gas Mark 8). Melt the butter in a small frying pan, add the ginger and 2 tablespoons caster sugar and cook over a low heat for 2 minutes.

2 Place the cream in a small saucepan and bring to the boil then remove from the heat immediately. Beat the egg yolks with the remaining 1 tablespoon caster sugar and slowly pour on the cream in a thin stream, whisking all the time. Finally add the ginger and sugar mixture and pour into an oval gratin dish.

3 Pour 3 cm (1¼ inches) of near-boiling water into a large metal roasting tin (pan) and set the dish containing the cream into it. Place in the oven and cook for 30 minutes, or until a blade inserted in the centre comes out clean. Leave to cool then chill for at least 4 hours, or preferably overnight.

4 When ready to serve, sprinkle the surface with the brown sugar and place under the grill (broiler) for about 2 minutes to caramelize it. Leave to cool for a few minutes before serving.

The most difficult part of producing this delicious dessert — which establishments from Catalonia to King's College, Cambridge, claim to have invented — is not caramelizing the sugar on the surface of the cream but removing it from the heat at the right moment. While China makes no claim on it, this basic cream made with eggs and caramelized sugar lends itself to all manner of interpretations.

Almond cream

Makes 12 small ramekins • **preparation** 15 minutes • **cooking** 30 minutes

40 g (⅜ cup) split almonds
1 vanilla pod (bean), split lengthways
115 g (½ cup) caster (superfine) sugar
5 egg yolks
250 ml (generous 1 cup) milk
250 ml (generous 1 cup) whipping cream

1 Preheat the oven to 180°C (350°F, Gas Mark 4). Spread the almonds on a baking sheet and roast them in the oven for 8 minutes, or until they are lightly browned. Leave to cool then pulverize them in a blender or food processor.

2 Scrape the inside of the vanilla pod to extract the seeds and mix them with the sugar. Beat the egg yolks and vanilla-flavoured sugar with an electric mixer until they are pale and creamy and fall in a ribbon from the beaters.

3 Place the vanilla pod, milk and the cream in a saucepan and bring to the boil. Remove the vanilla pod then pour the mixture on to the beaten egg mixture in a slow stream, whisking constantly. Stir in the ground almonds and pour the mixture into individual ramekins.

4 Pour a little near-boiling water into a large metal roasting tin (pan), set the ramekins into it and place in the oven. Cook for 30 minutes, or until the point of a knife inserted into the centre of the cream comes out clean.

One of my great dessert memories remains that of a hot sweet almond soup that was served at the end of a Chinese banquet. Since the first time I tasted them I have always adored almonds and they are still my favourite sweetmeat. I used them to flavour this delicious, very easy to prepare cream, which can be served hot or cold.

Lemon tart

Serves 6 • **preparation** 20 minutes • **cooking** 1 hour

For a tart tin (pan) about 26 cm (10¼ inches) in diameter

Pastry (pie dough)
110 g (generous ¾ cup) plain (all-purpose) flour, plus extra for dusting
55 g (generous ¼ cup) sugar
1 pinch salt
1 egg
90 g (6½ tablespoons) cold butter, or use ready-rolled store-bought shortcrust (unsweetened) pastry

Lemon cream
250 ml (generous 1 cup) whipping cream
2 whole eggs plus 1 yolk
115 g (½ cup) sugar
1 pinch salt
120 ml (½ cup) lemon juice
zest of 1 lemon

1 Place all the ingredients for the pastry in a large mixing bowl and work them into a smooth paste with your fingertips. Form into a ball and roll it on a lightly floured work surface, then wrap it in clingfilm (plastic wrap) and leave to chill for 30 minutes in the refrigerator.

2 Preheat the oven to 180°C (350°F, Gas Mark 4). Mix all the ingredients for the lemon cream together and set aside.

3 Roll out the pastry into a round (circle) 1.25 cm (½ inch) thick and lay it in the tart tin. Press it out with your fingers until it covers the base and sides of the tin. Cover with a sheet of foil weighted down with some dried beans and bake blind for 10 minutes. Remove the beans and foil, prick the pastry lightly all over with a fork and return to the oven for a further 8 minutes.

4 Pour the lemon cream into the partially baked pastry case (shell) and bake in the oven for 40 minutes, or until the cream is set and lightly browned. Leave to cool completely before serving.

Everyone in my family really enjoyed citrus fruit, especially in the form of refreshing orange slices eaten at the end of a meal — a dessert that was as light as it was healthy. Later, in France, when I discovered the wonderful world of fruit tarts, I naturally fell under the spell of citrus fruit tarts — orange or lemon. The lemon tart offered here is delicious and easy to make.

Mango ice cream
with crystallized ginger

Serves 4 • **preparation** 20 minutes • **cooking** 2–3 minutes

50 g (1¾ oz) fresh mango pulp
370 ml (generous 1½ cups) skimmed (skim) milk
2 tablespoons finely chopped crystallized (candied) ginger
3 egg yolks
55 g (generous ¼ cup) caster (superfine) sugar
1 tablespoon lemon juice

1 Pass the mango pulp through a fine sieve (strainer). Place the milk and crystallized ginger in a saucepan and bring to the boil, then remove from the heat.

2 Beat the egg yolks and sugar together with an electric mixer until the mixture is pale and creamy and falls in a ribbon from the beaters.

3 Incorporate the ginger-milk mixture a little at a time, whisking constantly. Return it to the saucepan and cook over a low heat for 2–3 minutes, stirring all the time with a wooden spoon. When the cream has thickened sufficiently to coat the back of the spoon, remove from the heat and leave to cool completely.

4 Mix the cream and the mango pulp together, pour into an ice cream machine and freeze according to the manufacturer's instructions. Alternatively, pour the mixture into a shallow, freezerproof container, cover and freeze for 2–3 hours until the mixture is partially frozen. Remove from the freezer, transfer to a bowl and break up the ice crystals with a fork. Return to the container and freeze for a further 2–3 hours. Repeat this process then freeze until firm.

The mango is an irreplaceable exotic fruit with a unique flavour. I added a little touch of crystallized ginger to make a fruity and sophisticated ice cream.

Basic recipes

Basic stock

Chicken stock

Fish stock

Turkey and poultry stock

Sauces

Tomato concassé

Tomato salsa with ginger

Mayonnaise with ginger and spring onions

Apple and plum sauce

Garlic mayonnaise with peppers and Sichuan pepper

Garlic mayonnaise with sesame seeds

Tomato-ginger sauce

'Mallard in a Vatel sauce — wine vinegar, egg yolk, tomato purée, butter, cream, salt and pepper, shallot, tarragon, chervil and peppercorns. Is there something there that you don't like?'

Rex Stout, *Nero Wolfe.*

Basic stock

Stock is an aid to cooking, seasoning and binding ingredients while at the same time uniting and improving the flavours. As its French name – *fond* – implies, it forms the basis of good cooking. A well-prepared stock can be compared to the foundations of a building, to money in the bank: always there to hand and turning a profit.

There is no great cuisine, in East or West, that does not insist on the quality of the stock used. In Japan, the *dashi* – the stock made from dried bonito and kelp – gives that country's cuisine its characteristic flavour. It is used in everything except chicken dishes. Japanese chefs maintain that the success of the dish depends on the quality of the *dashi* used to make it. Stock, of whatever kind, is an essential ingredient in almost all Chinese dishes. While it is indispensable in the preparation of soups (another key element of that country's cuisine) it

should not be confused with it (see Chicken Stock, page 218). Indeed, broth, stock and consommé are often seen as one and the same thing, but in fact this is not at all the case. Broth is the liquid in which ingredients that are intended for eating have been cooked – a pot-au-feu, for example. It is, in a way, a by-product that can be used in its own right. Clarified and enriched, it becomes consommé. Broth and consommé are a sort of dividend produced by cooking a dish, whereas stock – to extend the metaphor – is a capital deriving a profit from ingredients that would not otherwise be used. In a pot of classic stock are bird carcasses, meat bones and vegetable peelings, all simmering together to produce a tasty basis for sauces, gravies, jellies and soups. The different kinds of stock you will find in this chapter will not only serve as the basis of delicious soups but will improve and enhance any dishes to which you add them.

To help you make successful stock, the following are a few golden rules:

1 Stock must never boil – boiling will make it cloudy. It should simmer gently throughout the whole time it is cooking, preferably uncovered (covering it increases the likelihood of it overheating). Stock cooked at a gentle simmer will remain clear and transparent.

2 The most important operation when making stock or broth is skimming. It is also the most tedious. It maintains the clarity and flavour, and produces rich, clear and well-flavoured stock and is a small price to pay for such a worthwhile result. Use a large slotted spoon to remove the scum when it collects on the surface.

3 Wait until you have finished skimming before adding the vegetables, herbs and spices.

4 A word of warning: never stir the stock at any stage during cooking. The slightest movement within the stockpot will cloud the liquid.

5 Stock, once cooked, should be treated like wine and filtered or strained and decanted. Lift it out with a ladle, which should leave all the impurities at the bottom of the stockpot. I strain my stock through four thicknesses of muslin (cheesecloth).

6 Leave the stock to rest in a cool place then remove all the solidified fat and store in freezerproof containers in the freezer.

7 A final word on the ingredients, starting with chicken. While a tender young bird is a must when preparing chicken dishes, an old hen or cockerel is much better for making stock – and don't forget to include the feet (well cleaned and with claws removed). My chicken stock is used in a wide range of recipes, and you will encounter it regularly in this book. Why chicken? Because it produces a delicious, light, adaptable and cheap base,

easier to make than veal or beef stock which, by the way, is too strong for the average Chinese nose or palate. Perfectly suited to Chinese cooking, it is just as appropriate for Western cuisine. I use it not only as stock, but also reduced, in the form of a demi-glace, and to round off certain soups or dishes sautéed in a wok (such as Creamed Breast of Chicken with Red Peppers, page 118).

Pork broth is sometimes used in Chinese cooking, but chicken stock reigns supreme. It sometimes happens (as in Roast Pork with Chinese Spices, page 128) that the broth contains both chicken and pork. Fish and shellfish also make delicious stock, but it must be prepared and used separately. (See Fish Stock, page 219.) Fish bones release gelatine; cooked bones are also used on occasion.

8 Here are some ingredients that should be avoided in the preparation of stock: first of all, farinaceous vegetables, such as potatoes or dried pulses, which would make it cloudy. Likewise cabbage, turnips and other strongly flavoured vegetables should not be included because their strong taste would predominate.

Sauces

Cooks the world over are proud of their sauces, from garlic dressing to *hoisin* sauce via the Italian tomato and red (bell) pepper *salsa rossa*. A sauce is a preparation which should not be confused with a 'jus', which is simply the juices that have exuded from meat during cooking. Sauces should be an accompaniment, an enhancement, offering a contrast but never dominating.

The art of classic Western sauces began in France, influenced by the Italian Renaissance. La Varenne (around 1650) was the pioneer. Carême (around 1830) perfected the art, which attained its peak with Auguste Escoffier (around 1900). With the passage of time, French sauces have become the savoury and velvety accompaniment to a practically infinite number of culinary applications. Escoffier, in his *Guide Culinaire* (1902), which contained almost 200 sauces, explained: 'Sauces represent the most important aspect of cooking. They are the things that have created and maintained the universal preponderance of French cuisine.'

Indian, Chinese and Japanese cuisines are known for their original and tasty sauces, remarkable for containing neither flour nor eggs – ingredients found in traditional Western sauces, even though for the last 30 years, Nouvelle Cuisine has all but banned flour from them, favouring the use of reduced stocks, butter and cream in its place. Asian chefs tend to believe that Westerners drown the natural flavours of their food in sauces. Indeed, in Asia there is a preference for sauces to be served separately so food can be dipped in them according to personal taste. It is true, however, that classic French sauces are not intended to submerge the main ingredients. There is some truth on both sides.

In Asia, the art of making sauces is based on the judicious combination of spices and condiments and mixing them with vegetable oils, stock and wine. They can be aromatic, biting, acid, bland, sweet, spiced, bitter, subtle or all those at the same time. Whatever goes into their makeup, they share with Western sauces the purpose of underlining, enhancing and deepening the flavour of the dish they accompany.

The recipes for sauces that you will find in this book are the result of my experience of merging the culinary principles and tastes of both East and West. For example, Mayonnaise with Ginger and Spring Onions (page 223) contains two popular and traditional Chinese condiments. These are never added to mayonnaise in the West, and mayonnaise itself is a stranger to Asian kitchens. All these sauces, in their own way, seek to represent that 'most important aspect' of the cuisine so dear to Escoffier.

Chicken stock

Makes 7.5 litres (8 quarts) • **preparation** 30 minutes • **cooking** 5–6 hours

1 boiling fowl weighing
about 2.5 kg (5 lb 8 oz)
or 1 chicken of the same size
and 3.5 kg (8 lb) raw poultry
bones (carcasses, feet)
8 litres (scant 8½ quarts)
cold water
1 kg (2 lb 4 oz) carrots,
peeled and thickly sliced
500 g (1 lb 2 oz) onions, peeled
3 heads garlic
4 fresh thyme sprigs or
2 teaspoons dried thyme
3 bay leaves
1 tablespoon coarse salt
2 tablespoons black peppercorns
2 cloves

1 Place the chicken and bones in a large stockpot. Add the water and bring slowly to the boil. Skim frequently until the surface is clear. Add the vegetables, herbs, salt and spices. Leave to simmer very slowly for 5–6 hours, skimming whenever necessary.

2 Using a slotted spoon, lift out the chicken, bones and vegetables. Line a colander with several layers of butter muslin (cheesecloth) and strain the stock through it. Leave to cool completely then leave to stand in the cool place until the fat has solidified on the surface. Remove the fat and pour the stock into freezerproof containers with tight-fitting lids and store in the freezer.

Your chicken stock can never be better than the ingredients that have gone into making it. Everything, including the old boiling fowl, must be just as fresh as those you would choose to put in any dish. If the quantities given here are too great, reduce them by half.

Fish stock

Makes 4 litres (scant 4¼ quarts) • **preparation** 15 minutes • **cooking** 1 hour

4.5 kg (10 lb) bones and heads
from firm-fleshed fish
4 litres (scant 4¼ quarts)
cold water
250 g (9 oz) onions, peeled and
coarsely chopped
500 g (1 lb 2 oz) carrots, peeled
and coarsely chopped
120 g (4¼ oz) shallots, peeled
and coarsely chopped
2 leeks (white part only),
coarsely chopped
1 small bunch fresh flat-leaf
parsley
4 fresh thyme sprigs or
2 teaspoons dried thyme
2 bay leaves
4 garlic cloves, unpeeled
but lightly crushed
1 tablespoon black peppercorns
coarse salt

1 Rinse the fish bones and heads under cold running water then place them in a large stockpot, cover with the water and bring to a simmer. Cook for 10 minutes, skimming regularly. Add the rest of the ingredients and simmer slowly for 1 hour.

2 Lift out the bones and vegetables with a slotted spoon, strain the stock through a colander lined with several layers of butter muslin (cheesecloth), leave it to cool then skim the surface again. Pour the stock into small freezerproof containers with tight-fitting lids and store in the freezer.

Fish stock is not traditionally used in Chinese cooking. It was in France that I discovered its virtues. It is easier and quicker to make than chicken stock but the rules are the same for both — it must not come to a full boil. Once frozen it will keep for a long time, you will have it to hand to make dishes and sauces based on fish and shellfish. Here too, if the quantities are too great, reduce them by half.

Turkey and poultry stock

Makes 7 litres (generous 7⅓ quarts) • **preparation** 30 minutes • **cooking** 7 hours

1 raw turkey carcass

1 chicken weighing about 3 kg (6 lb 8 oz) or 2 hens weighing 1.5 kg (3 lb 5 oz)

1 kg (2 lb 4 oz) chicken giblets (necks, carcasses, wings, feet)

8 litres (scant 8½ quarts) cold water

1.25 kg (2 lb 12 oz) carrots, peeled and halved lengthways

4 onions, peeled and cut into halves

3 leeks (white part only), washed

4 heads garlic

8 fresh thyme sprigs or 4 teaspoons dried thyme

3 bay leaves

1 teaspoon coarse salt

2 tablespoons peppercorns

1 Place the turkey carcass, chicken and giblets in a large stockpot and cover with the water. Bring to simmering point, skim several times until nothing more rises to the surface, then add the vegetables, herbs, salt and peppercorns. Leave to simmer for 7 hours, skimming regularly.

2 Lift out the carcass, the chicken and giblets with a slotted spoon. Strain the stock through a colander lined with several layers of butter muslin (cheesecloth). Leave it to cool then leave to chill in the refrigerator. Remove the solidified fat from the surface, pour the stock into small freezerproof containers with tight-fitting lids and store in the freezer.

This is not a stock to use in everyday cooking. More trouble than Chicken Stock (page 218), it has a marvellously rich aroma and is more suited to a festive meal. You could make it more cheaply by replacing all or some of the whole chicken, but use chicken or boiling fowl in some form or another as turkey alone does not give a rich enough flavour.
Follow the advice given in the Chicken Stock recipe; you will obtain a stock of excellent quality to make sauces, gravies and delicious consommés. It can even be eaten as it is. If you wish to enrich a sauce, such as that for Boned and Roasted Turkey *(page 94), you need only reduce it in order to concentrate its flavour. No need for flour or other thickeners. This stock must be prepared at least a day in advance. If any is left, freeze it.*

Tomato concassé

1.5–2 kg (3 lb 5 oz–4 lb 8 oz) ripe tomatoes
1 tablespoon granulated sugar
2 tablespoons extra virgin olive oil
salt and freshly ground black pepper

1 Peel the tomatoes after blanching them for a few seconds. Remove the seeds then chop the flesh with a knife. Sprinkle on the sugar and leave to drain in a stainless steel or enamelled colander for 20–25 minutes. Sponge them with kitchen paper (paper towels) to eliminate the excess moisture.

2 For hot tomato concassé, heat the olive oil in a sauté pan, add the tomatoes and cook for 2 minutes. Season with salt and pepper and serve.

The tomatoes here are sprinkled with sugar to get rid of the excess moisture and at the same time bring out the quintessential flavour of the tomato. Tomato concassé can be used for numerous preparations. It can serve as a sauce for Whole Fish Fried Crisp with Tomatoes *(page 64), to garnish* Steamed Scallops *(page 59) or as the basis for* Cubed Tomatoes with Tarragon and Sesame Oil *(page 38). It can also serve as a sauce for pasta with grated cheese.*

Tomato salsa
with ginger

Makes about 600 ml (2½ cups) • **preparation** 5 minutes

500 ml (generous 2 cups)
Tomato Concassé (page 221)
2 teaspoons finely chopped
fresh root ginger
2 tablespoons finely chopped
spring onions (scallions)
1 tablespoon fresh red chillies
(chilies), de-seeded and
finely chopped
2 tablespoons finely chopped
fresh coriander (cilantro)
2 tablespoons lime juice
salt and freshly ground
black pepper

1 Mix all the ingredients together in a bowl, cover and leave to chill for 1 hour in the refrigerator. Serve cold or at room temperature.

This recipe was inspired by Mexican cuisine — one of my favourites — and in it the traditional fresh tomato sauce is given a final bite by the addition of ginger, which gives it a special dimension. This sauce is ideal with fried dishes, whose richness is balanced by the interesting contrast it makes to their crunchy texture. You could serve it with Whole Fish Fried Crisp with Tomatoes *(page 64).*

Mayonnaise with ginger and spring onions

Makes about 250 ml (generous 1 cup) • **preparation** 5 minutes

3 large egg yolks
1 teaspoon fine salt
freshly ground white pepper
½ teaspoon ginger juice
1 teaspoon lemon juice
2 tablespoons finely chopped
spring onions (scallions)
80 ml (5½ tablespoons) olive oil
120 ml (½ cup) groundnut
(peanut) oil

1 All the ingredients must be at room temperature. In a blender or food processor, beat the egg yolks with the salt and pepper. Add the ginger juice, lemon juice and the spring onions then gradually add the olive oil in a thin continuous stream until it is completely incorporated in the mixture. Add the groundnut oil in the same way and continue beating until the mayonnaise is thick. Pour into a container with a tight-fitting lid and store in the refrigerator until needed.

2 A word of advice: my way of making mayonnaise is easy and practically foolproof. However, if the mayonnaise should curdle, you need only add 1 tablespoon of hot water to 1 tablespoon of mayonnaise in a clean bowl and continue to beat it, adding the rest of the mayonnaise a little at a time. Your sauce will be saved.

Mayonnaise adapts itself to all whims and fantasies. Its basic ingredients — egg yolks and oil — accept any additions, all condiments, herbs and spices, to produce an infinite number of new flavours. It is limited only by the bounds of your imagination, the ingredients available and the requirements of the dish it is to accompany. This sauce is the result of the meeting of two concepts: in Asia, ginger and spring onions regularly come together in sauces, so all that is needed is the addition of Western mayonnaise. Ginger and spring onions are the perfect flavourings for pork, chicken and, above all, shellfish (see Grilled Crab and Lobster, (page 58) You could give it a nutty flavour by using 2 tablespoons of sesame oil instead of the olive oil, and increasing the quantity of groundnut oil to 180 ml (generous ¾ cup).

Apple and plum sauce

Makes about 350 ml (1½ cups) • **preparation** 15 minutes

1 kg (2 lb 4 oz) Golden
Delicious apples
1 teaspoon lemon juice
1 tablespoon granulated sugar
freshly ground black pepper
120 ml (½ cup) plum sauce
water

1 Peel and core the apples and cut into cubes about 2.5 cm (1 inch). Place them in a saucepan with the lemon juice then add the sugar and pepper and pour in enough water to cover the apples. Simmer, uncovered, over a low heat for 10 minutes.

2 Drain the apples in a sieve (strainer) and place them in a blender. Add the plum sauce and blend to a purée. Leave to cool completely then store in the refrigerator until needed.

Plum sauce is a traditional Chinese ingredient made from plums and apricots preserved in vinegar with sugar and chilli (chili). Thick and spicy, it is packed in cans or jars. Combining it with apple compote gives a light, smooth and delicately spiced sauce. It can be prepared in advance and stored in the refrigerator. It goes very well with pork (for example Pork Roasted with Chinese Spices on page 128) and with Boned and Roasted Turkey (page 94) — in fact with any dish that can be served with a fruity, acidic condiment. Trust your taste and your experience. I use Golden Delicious apples, which are readily available and perfectly suitable for both sweet and savoury dishes.

Garlic mayonnaise with peppers and Sichuan pepper

Makes about 250 ml (generous 1 cup) • **preparation** 20 minutes

120 g (4¼ oz) large fresh
red (bell) peppers
2 egg yolks
1 tablespoon finely chopped garlic
1 teaspoon salt flavoured
with Sichuan pepper
(glossary, page 237)
salt and freshly ground
white pepper
2 tablespoons fresh orange juice
120 ml (½ cup) olive oil
120 ml (½ cup) groundnut
(peanut) oil

1 Roast the peppers over a gas flame or under the grill (broiler), turning them frequently, until the surface is totally blackened. Remove them to a plastic bag, seal and leave to stand for 15 minutes, then remove the peppers from the bag, cut them in half and remove the skin and seeds. Chop the flesh finely and set aside.

2 Place the pepper flesh, egg yolks, garlic, salt flavoured with Sichuan pepper, salt, pepper and orange juice in a blender or mortar and reduce to a fine paste. Gradually add the olive oil in a thin continuous stream until it is completely incorporated in the mixture. Add the groundnut oil in the same way and continue beating until the mayonnaise is thick and perfectly blended. Note: the sauce will not be as thick as ordinary mayonnaise.

This sauce is an East—West version of the Provençal 'rouille', which is served with bouillabaisse and which the fishermen of Martigues swear is an aphrodisiac. They even go as far as to say that, while bouillabaisse itself possesses that quality, the addition of rouille multiplies the effect by one hundred. And this version, combining mayonnaise and Sichuan pepper — which adds a singular flavour reminiscent of lavender — is even more inflammatory. It is an excellent accompaniment for Fish Stew Flavoured with Ginger *(page 78) and* Poached Fillets of Fish with Ginger *(page 62).*

Garlic mayonnaise
with sesame seeds

Makes about 250 ml (generous 1 cup) • **preparation** 10 minutes

2 egg yolks
2 tablespoons finely
chopped garlic
2 teaspoons white Japanese
or Chinese rice vinegar
salt and freshly ground
white pepper
1 tablespoon sesame oil
120 ml (½ cup) olive oil
120 ml (½ cup) groundnut
(peanut) oil
4 tablespoons finely chopped
spring onions (scallions)
1 tablespoon toasted sesame
seeds

1 Blend the egg yolks with the garlic, vinegar, salt and pepper in a blender or food processor. Mix the three oils together in a small jug (pitcher) and slowly add them in a thin continuous stream, processing constantly until they are completely incorporated. Add the chopped spring onions then transfer the mayonnaise to a bowl and stir in the sesame seeds.

Aïoli, since my stay in the South of France, has become one of my passions. Faithful to my Asian heritage, I have added sesame seeds and rice vinegar to this mayonnaise, giving it a 'crunchy' texture that spices up dishes without overwhelming them.

Bok Choy

This type of cabbage comes from southern China. Its stalks are thick and crisp and slightly sweet. Its round, green leaves have a sweetish flavour somewhat similar to spinach. To prepare it, cut the leaves and peel the stalks then slice them finely across their thickness. Wash them carefully.

Butter

I always like to use the best quality butter. In my recipes it always refers to unsalted butter. Butter can be stored in the freezer and thawed out as needed.

Chilli bean paste *see Beans**

Chillies (chilies) and peppers (hot)

In Chinese cuisine, the very hot, small red dried chilli, about 5 cm (2 inches) long, is used more than any other kind. In Asian food stores you can also buy the shorter, thinner and very aromatic fresh red or green peppers used in Vietnamese and Thai cooking. There is a particular Thai variety, which is short and rounded and very hot. Chilli oil is also available and serves to flavour foods cooked in a wok. Finally, chilli sauce contains garlic and is mostly used as a condiment at the table. See also under *Beans (Chilli bean paste)**.

Chinese sausages

Several types of dried sausage come under this heading: Chinese sausages themselves, Vietnamese sausages (*lap xuang*) or Thai sausages, flavoured with rice alcohol or lemon grass. All slightly sweetish, generally based on pork (but sometimes also on beef or duck liver), they are delicious and must be cooked before being eaten. They can be sautéed or blanched until the fat just becomes translucent, which makes them lighter. If you plan to eat them within two weeks, store them in the refrigerator. To keep for a longer period, wrap them carefully and store in the freezer.

Tomato-ginger sauce

Makes about 1 litre (4 cups) • **preparation** 5 minutes • **cooking** 25 minutes

3 tablespoons extra virgin olive oil
6 tablespoons finely chopped onion
4 tablespoons finely chopped spring onions (scallions)
1 tablespoon finely chopped fresh root ginger
1 litre (4 cups) Tomato Concassé (page 221)
3 garlic cloves, lightly crushed
salt and freshly ground black pepper

1 Heat the olive oil in a saucepan. Add the onion, spring onions and ginger then reduce the heat and leave them to sweat until the onion has become translucent. Add the Tomato Concassé, garlic, salt and pepper and cook, uncovered, over a low heat for 25 minutes.

Fresh tomatoes – preferably the bright red and full-flavoured ones grown in the summer – well reduced to a thick coulis, flavoured with ginger, onion, spring onions, butter and garlic, is the best possible sauce for pasta or, for example, for Fresh Corn and Spring Onion Soufflé *(page 178).*

Glossary of ingredients

Note: Asterisks are cross references to other entries in the glossary.

Basil

There are European and Asian varieties of basil. While they differ subtly in flavour, they are more or less interchangeable. Asian or Thai basil, however, which is widely used in Vietnam and Thailand, seems to me to be stronger, with more of a bite. The aniseed (anise) flavour is delicious and I use it frequently in my East–West cuisine. Washed and dried, the leaves can be stored in good-quality olive oil. They blacken quickly when exposed to the air. Always use fresh basil; it loses its flavour when dried and adds little to the dish.

Beans

Bean sauce: *see Sauce.**

Chilli (chili) bean paste

Chilli paste, made from chillies and salt, often has black bean paste added to it (chilli black bean paste) or soya beans (soybeans), sometimes with garlic. The variety to use is specified in the recipes. Store it in an airtight jar in the refrigerator.

Fermented black beans

These little black soya beans (soybeans), fermented with a mixture of salt and spices, can be bought in cans, jars or plastic sachets. Their strong, salty taste is often mixed with ginger and garlic to make delicious sauces. Do not wash them, and be careful about adding salt as they are already very salty. Also use them sparingly – too much could spoil a dish. Chop them coarsely to release their spicy flavour. They keep for a long time at room temperature, but the container must be airtight.

Coriander (cilantro), fresh

Sometimes known as Arab parsley or Chinese parsley in France, coriander is very similar in appearance to flat-leaf parsley, and is now widely available. This herb is used fresh in all kinds of hot and cold dishes; its refreshing, aromatic and musky flavour is unique. Buy it as fresh as possible, with shiny, unblemished leaves. It will keep for several days if washed and drained, then wrapped in kitchen paper (paper towels) and covered with clingfilm (plastic wrap). Alternatively, place in a plastic bag and store in the refrigerator.

Cream

Generally speaking, being a dairy product, cream is not used in Chinese cooking. However, I do use it in some of my East–West recipes to enrich their flavour and reinforce their texture. When crème fraîche (or sour cream) is not specified, use single (light) or whipping cream.

Dried tomatoes

Generally imported from Italy, these sun-dried tomatoes have a pungent and acidic flavour. They are sold either in their natural state or preserved in olive oil. Store them in a cool dark place or even in the refrigerator.

Five-spice

This specifically Chinese spice mixture consists of *star anise** and *Sichuan pepper**, as well as fennel, cloves and Chinese cinnamon. It is easy to find in powdered form, in small amounts. Its sweet and aniseed (anise) flavours perform miracles in marinades, but use it sparingly because it is very strong. It will keep for a long time in an airtight jar.

Garlic shoots

These shoots are gathered before the plant has had time to form a bulb and they are rather like spring onions (scallions) but finer and lighter in colour. Use them chopped, like chives, in delicate dishes. See *Spring onions**.

Ginger

This irregularly shaped, bulbous rhizome is readily available fresh. In some Asian food stores you can even find 'green ginger', a very young, pinkish-white ginger that is so delicate it does not need peeling. Ripe ginger should be firm, shiny and covered with a smooth, golden skin that must be scraped off before use. It will keep for about two weeks in the salad compartment of the refrigerator. To keep it for longer, peel it and chop it into large pieces, place in a jar and cover with *rice wine**. Seal the jar and store in the refrigerator. With fish and shellfish, ginger takes on a similar role to lemon; it is also used to flavour oils, sauces and many dishes. It goes well with even the most bitter vegetables, to which it gives a touch of spice and freshness. It gives a remarkable strength of flavour to marinades. To make ginger juice (one of the ingredients found in my recipes), grate it finely, wrap it in a piece of cloth or place it in a very fine sieve (strainer) and squeeze it firmly, collecting the juice.

Hoisin: *see Sauce**.

Kumquats

This citrus fruit is like a tiny, elongated orange. The whole of the fruit is edible and tastes bitter and acidic at the same time. They are available fresh or crystallized (candied).

Lemon grass

Lemon grass is a tropical herb with a strong lemon and slightly camphor aroma. More commonly used in South-east Asia than in China, it is available fresh (or already chopped and frozen) in Asian food stores. Use only the swollen bulb, the tenderest part of the stem, and discard the outer leaves. Lightly crush the bulb (to release the aromas) before chopping it as finely as possible (because of its fibrous texture). Lemon grass will keep for up to six weeks in a plastic bag in the salad compartment of the refrigerator.

Mushrooms

Black mushrooms

These Chinese dried mushrooms (Judas ears) have a crunchy consistency and smell slightly of humus. They need to be soaked in hot water until they soften, then the woody ends of the stalks should be cut off and the mushrooms washed carefully to eliminate all traces of sand. They will keep for a long time in an airtight jar. There are two varieties: shredded ones, which are quite cheap, and the more expensive whole ones ('mushroom flowers'), large and full of cracks, whitish in colour or light beige. When soaked they become thick and velvety. The shredded kind are fine for dishes that require them chopped or minced; keep the others for those times when serving them whole will improve the appearance and texture of the dish. Both types are sold in clear plastic sachets.

Enokitake

These are little white mushrooms with long stalks, originally from Japan, and can be found in Asian food stores. Heated (they should be barely cooked), they take on a slightly viscous texture and a faint flavour of hazelnuts. Wash them, trim the base of the stalks then wrap them in damp kitchen paper (paper towels) and cover with clingfilm (plastic wrap). Keep them in the salad compartment of the refrigerator.

Oyster mushrooms

These cultivated mushrooms have a sweet and delicate flavour. Keep them in the refrigerator, like the enokitake.

Shiitake

The aromatic Chinese mushrooms or shiitake, are now cultivated in Europe and America and can be bought fresh. The dried ones that come from China or Japan are less delicate than the fresh ones but their aroma is much more developed. You will find these dried ones already chopped, in clear plastic sachets.

Noodles

Noodles made from wheat flour

Made from soft or hard wheat flour and water, Chinese noodles are sold either fresh or dried. They come in a number of varieties. Generally, the flat noodles are served in soups and the round ones in fried or sautéed dishes.

Rice noodles

Noodles made from rice flour must be softened for 15 minutes or so in very hot water. To keep them after they are soaked, drain them thoroughly, toss them in a little sesame oil and store in the refrigerator.

Nuoc-Mâm: *see Fish sauce**.

Oil

Groundnut (peanut) oil

This is the oil I prefer for cooking in a wok and deep-frying, because it has a neutral flavour and a high smoke point. Corn, soya (soy) or sunflower oils can be used as substitutes. Store it in a cool dark place.

Olive oil

The best olive oil is unfiltered and comes from the first cold pressing. It contains less than 1 per cent acidity. Its flavour is mild and fruity. Store it tightly sealed in a cool place.

Sesame oil

The Chinese form of this oil, with its rich, hazelnut flavour, is made from toasted sesame seeds. It is intended for use in dressings, not for cooking; it must not be heated. Dark and thick, it burns easily and should be added in the very last stages of the cooking. It is sometimes added to soups just before serving. In small amounts it adds a strong flavour of hazelnuts to a marinade. Diluted with a more neutral oil, it makes an original vinaigrette for salads and fresh pasta. Raw sesame oil, imported from India and the Middle East, is available in organic food stores, but it is not suitable for Chinese cooking as it is not sufficiently aromatic.

Oysters: *see Sauce**.

Pastry for Chinese ravioli (*wonton skins*)

You will find these thin wrappers of wheat flour pastry, sold in square packets, among the fresh produce in Asian food stores. They are used to make Chinese ravioli (*wonton*). They don't keep for long in the refrigerator, so use them within a week of buying them. They are also available frozen, but make sure they are thoroughly thawed before using.

Peppers: *see Chillies**.

Pig's caul (caul fat)

This is the fatty membrane that encloses the intestines of a pig and may be ordered from your local butcher. It is used to wrap ingredients to keep them soft and moist during cooking. It can be stored in the freezer in a suitably airtight container.

Plum: *see Sauce**.

Rice

Among the numerous varieties of rice on the market, the two principal types are long-grain and round. If you use long-grain rice there is no need to soak it. Among the long-grain kinds my favourites are basmati and jasmine-perfumed Thai rice (jasmine rice). Asian round rice, often from Japan, is marketed under the names of *Pearl rice* or *Japanese Rose*. With its little, pearly round grains, it is generally used for stuffings and desserts.

Rice flour pastry sheets

These Vietnamese pastry sheets, made from rice flour (*banh trang*), are used in the preparation of spring rolls (*cha gio*) and *nems*. Finer and crisper than the Asian wheat version (spring roll wrappers), they come in two sizes. They keep almost indefinitely and must be softened in warm water before use.

Rice noodles: *see Noodles**

Rice wine

The wine known as 'Shaoxing rice wine' is made in China from fermented rice. Amber in colour, it has a rich aroma, soft and complex. You could replace it with dry sherry (but not with *sake*, which has a very different flavour). When buying, do not confuse the wine intended for drinking (*Shaoxing wine*) – sold under a pale blue or red label – with the red label one specially produced for use in the kitchen (*Shaoxing cooking wine*). *Mirin* is a sweet Japanese sake intended for cooking. Opened bottles should be stored at room temperature.

Salt

For the most part, I prefer to use pure and delicate natural fine salt. Coarse sea salt has too strong a flavour.

Chinese salt flavoured with Sichuan pepper

I borrowed the traditional Chinese recipe for this but made a few small changes. It works wonders even in Western dishes – such as *Roast Pork with Chinese spices* on page 128 – and anywhere where a lively, spicy touch is required (such as *Steamed Scallops*, page 59). Sichuan pepper gives this salt its bite and slightly piquant length on the palate, qualities peculiar to Sichuan cooking. Personally, this aroma reminds me of coriander seeds and lavender from Provence, but no other spices can replace Sichuan pepper. Happily, it is becoming easier and easier to find in Asian food stores or good grocery stores.

This is the way I make Chinese salt flavoured with Sichuan pepper (to make about 6 tablespoons): in a dry wok or a cast-iron sauté pan, heat 4 tablespoons of Sichuan pepper and 2 tablespoons of fine salt or grey sea salt. As soon as the pan is very hot, reduce the heat and shake the ingredients for 1 minute, or until the Sichuan pepper colours (don't let it burn). Remove from the heat and leave to cool, then grind the mixture coarsely in a blender. Store in an airtight jar.

Sauces

Bean sauce

This is called by several names: Bean Sauce, Brown Bean Paste, Yellow Bean Sauce. In its various forms this paste, made from soya beans (soybeans), flour, salt and water, is used to enrich braised dishes. The beans are either whole, crushed or puréed. I prefer sauce containing whole beans, which is less salty than the others. If you buy it in a can, transfer it to an airtight glass jar and store it in the refrigerator, where it will keep indefinitely.

Fish sauce

The Vietnamese call it *Nuoc-mâm* and in Thailand it is *nam pla*: It is basically the same sauce, sold in bottles or small jars. Made from fish that has been soaked in saline then fermented, it has a characteristic aroma of the sea and lends a rich aroma when added to dishes. In the cooking of South-east Asia it plays the same role as that of *Soy sauce** in Chinese cuisine.

Hoisin sauce

Extensively used in southern China and South-east Asia, hoisin sauce is made from soya (soy) flour, red kidney beans, chilli (chili), sugar, salt, garlic and spices. It is thick, with a flavour that is sweet and hot at the same time. It is generally sold in glass jars, which need to be kept cool after they are opened. It keeps almost indefinitely and is delicious in marinades or as a sauce at the table.

Lemon sauce

This is a thick sauce, made from lemon, salt and sugar and sold in jars. It is not unlike the fruit chutneys used in Indian cooking. Peculiar to Cantonese cuisine, it is delicious in braised dishes. Once opened, it should be stored in a cool place.

Oyster sauce

Typical of southern China, this sauce, made from oysters, salt and spices has a rich flavour reminiscent of meat cooking juices. The more expensive brands tend to be the best. Store in the refrigerator.

Plum sauce

This traditional Chinese condiment is bought in cans or jars. It is made from plums, crystallized (candied) ginger, chilli (chili), vinegar and sugar. In Chinese restaurants it is served as it is, with duck; diluted, it is used to season such dishes as fried rolls, meatballs or fried *wonton* (ravioli). Fruity, spicy, full of character, plum sauce added to a braising sauce gives delicious results.

Soy sauce

This liquid brown sauce is the result of fermenting soya beans (soybean) and cereals (usually wheat, but sometimes rye). It comes in two main types – light soy sauce and spicy soy sauce. Light soy sauce is saltier and used in cooking; you may find it under the label of 'Superior Soy Sauce'. Spicy soy sauce is darker, thicker and has a more pronounced aroma. It serves mostly for braised dishes and on the table as a condiment. I am particularly fond of the Japanese sauce *Kikkoman®* and recommend it for its excellent quality and the natural way it is made. Mushroom Soy Sauce is somewhere between the light and the spicy sauces, with the added juice of straw mushrooms. All soy sauces keep well at room temperature.

Sesame

Sesame paste

Sesame paste is rich, thick and creamy brown, made from toasted sesame seeds. It should not be confused with *tahina* or *tahini*, Mediterranean versions made with raw seeds still with their skins. You can buy sesame paste in pots in Asian food stores and it is used in both hot and cold dishes. One could, if necessary, use peanut butter instead. See also *Oil**.

Shiitake: see *Mushrooms**.

Sichuan pepper

This is not a true pepper but the dried red berries of a Chinese bush, which have a strong, peppery smell and a very characteristic astringent flavour. Roast them briefly in the oven, or a dry frying pan, grind them in a clean coffee mill and store the powder in an airtight jar. In that way you will have the spice ready for use.

Soya (soy)

Soy sauce: *see Sauce**.

Soya vermicelli

These very fine vermicelli are made from mungo beans, starch and water. In their dry state they are thin, brittle and an opaque white in colour; when soaked they swell and become transparent. They are used to thicken soups and to give bulk to stuffings.

Spring onions, young onions (scallions)

Spring onions and young onions are fresh flavourings that, together with ginger and garlic, are the three key ingredients in Chinese cooking. Young onions are tiny, round and white, whereas spring onions look more like miniature leeks and are a different species. Both these plants impart a delicate onion flavour to many dishes. To prepare them, remove the outside layers, the roots and the green part. The bulbs can be finely sliced or cut into julienne strips as a garnish. The green part gives a touch of colour as well as flavour. When the recipes in this book call for spring onions, you could equally well use young onions or young shallots. See also *Garlic (shoots)**.

Star Anise

The dried fruit of the anise or badiane tree, a member of the Illiciaceae family native to East Asia, takes the form of an eight-pointed star. Star anise is one of the components of Chinese five-spice* but is also used whole. It confers a rich, liquorice flavour to braised dishes. It is sold in plastic sachets, but should be stored in an airtight jar.

Sugar

In Chinese cooking, sugar is used to balance salty and spicy flavours. You will find several kinds of raw sugar in Asian food stores: cane sugar, malt or palm sugar (jaggery), brown or yellow, granulated or in lumps that need to be wrapped in a cloth and broken with a hammer. You can replace them with granulated or brown sugar.

Vermicelli: see *Soya**.

Vinegar

Chinese vinegars are generally made from rice or sometimes sorghum. They offer a wide range of flavours, from sweet to very acidic. You could use cider vinegar in their place, but you should not have any great difficulty in finding them in Asian food stores and they will keep for a long time at room temperature. White rice vinegar is much more delicate than ordinary white vinegar; it does wonders for sweet and sour dishes. If you can't find any vinegar of Chinese origin you could use the Japanese brand *Mitsukan®*. Chinese black vinegar (known as *Chinkiang Vinegar*) is dark and opaque and seems more strongly flavoured than it really is. Its flavour is very much like balsamic vinegar, possibly because it is made in a similar way. It is delicious in braised dishes or in sauces. The slightly sweet red rice vinegar is usually served with seafood.

Water chestnuts

About the size of a walnut, this edible fruit of an aquatic plant (Latin name *Trapa natans*) is incorrectly called a 'chestnut'. When fresh, they are crunchy and sweet. They should have a smooth skin and be firm when tested with a fingernail. Unpeeled, they can be kept for about two weeks in the refrigerator, wrapped in paper. Once peeled, they should be immersed in water and stored in a cool place. They are easier to find preserved in cans or jars, but the process robs them of their flavour. Rinse them under cold running water before using; any surplus can be kept for several days in the refrigerator providing the water is changed regularly.

Young onions: see *Spring onions**.

East–West menus

Here are a few examples of dishes combined to form a meal. Obviously everything is possible, so set your imagination free and ... Bon Appétit!

Christmas menu

Boned and roasted turkey, rice stuffing with herbs, reduced cooking juices (pages 94–95)

Potato purée with spring onions (page 174)

Apple and plum sauce   (page 224)

Sugar snap peas sautéed with carrots (page 175)

Mandarin sorbet (page 194) or fresh fruit

Summer barbecue

Grilled crab and lobster, mayonnaise with ginger and spring onions (pages 58 and 223)

Spatchcocked marinated pigeon with Shaoxing rice wine sauce (page 120)

Cubed tomatoes with tarragon and sesame oil (page 38)

Summer vegetables sautéed with black Chinese vinegar (page 190)

Warm peach compote with basil (page 206)

Provençal flavours (with a Chinese touch)

Cold tomato and lemon grass soup (page 49)

Roast rack of lamb marinated in a Chinese style (page 133)

Chinese ratatouille (page 179)

Almond cream (page 210)

For duck lovers

Duck salad with the flavours of Asia (page 35)

Duck served as two courses (page 112)

Lemon tart (page 211)

Easy but stylish menu

Soup with goat's cheese *wonton* (page 48)

Steamed fish with tomatoes and basil (page 60)

Spatchcocked marinated pigeon with Shaoxing rice wine sauce (page 120)

Green salad

Fresh fruit in season

Elegant menu to astonish your guests

Oyster consommé (page 50)

Salmon wrapped in Chinese cabbage leaves and steamed (page 72)

Roast pork with Chinese spices (page 128)

Mango ice cream with crystallized ginger (page 212)

Simple, light menu

Steamed scallops (page 59)

Vegetable spaghetti (page 176)

Tomato salad with ginger and spring onion vinaigrette (page 39)

Fresh fruit in season

Index of recipes in alphabetical order

Acknowledgements

Ken Hom 'I am profoundly grateful to Sophie Brissaud for her work on the translation and editorial adaptation of this book; to Mickaël Roulier and Emmanuel Turiot for their magnificent work on the photography and design; to my dear friend Giacomo Bretzel who has managed to capture the ideal atmosphere with his photographs. And, of course, to Brigitte Éveno, Florence Feisthauer and Raphaële Huard for the editing; to Dune Lunel for the layout and finally, of course, to Pierre-Jean Furet and Stephen Bateman who had the inspired idea of publishing this book. My warmest thanks to them all.
A little word of thanks, too, to the team that worked with me on the first edition of this book; particularly to Gerry Cavanaugh, Gordon Wing, Martha Casselman and Ted Lyman.'

Mickaël Roulier would like to thank Nathanaël Turpin-Griset for his invaluable help.

Emmanuel Turiot wishes to thank the Muji boutiques and the Compagnie Française de l'Orient et de la Chine for the loan of the items that are shown in the illustrations; also Géraldine Sauvage for her invaluable help.

Management, Stephen Bateman and Pierre-Jean Furet
Editor in chief, Brigitte Éveno
Graphic design and implementation, Dune Lunel (Modzilla!)
Editorial follow-up, Florence Feisthauer
Production, Claire Leleu

The editor would like to thank Raphaële Huard for her invaluable help and meticulous re-editing.

Photo-engraving by Reproscan, Italy

First published by Hachette Pratique, an imprint of Hachette-Livre
43 Quai de Grenelle, Paris 75905, Cedex 15, France
Under the title *Le meilleur de ma cuisine: Wok & Co*
© 2004, Editions du Chêne – Hachette Livre
All rights reserved

English language translation produced by Translate-A-Book, Oxford

This edition published by Hachette Illustrated UK, Octopus Publishing Group,
2–4 Heron Quays, London, E14 4JP
English Translation © 2004, Octopus Publishing Group Ltd, London

ISBN 10: 1 84430 177 X
ISBN 13: 978 1 84430 177 5
Printed by Toppan Printing Co., (HK) Ltd.